A-Z REDDITCH & KIDDER...

CW00428240

Key to Map Pages	2-3
Map Pages	4-36

Index t...
Villages...
and sel...

REFERENCE

Motorway	**M42**
A Road	**A441**
B Road	**B4091**
Dual Carriageway	
One-way Street Traffic flow on A Roads is also indicated by a heavy line on the driver's left.	→
Road Under Construction Opening dates are correct at the time of publication.	
Proposed Roads	
Restricted Access	
Pedestrianized Road	
Track / Footpath	-----
Residential Walkway	....
Railway	Level Crossing / Station / Tunnel / Heritage Station
Built-up Area	HILL / ST.
Local Authority Boundary	— · — · —
Posttown Boundary	— — —
Postcode Boundary (within Posttown)	— — —
Map Continuation	**28**
Car Park (selected)	**P**

Church or Chapel	†
Cycleway (selected)	🚲 ·······
Fire Station	■
Hospital	**H**
House Numbers (A & B Roads only)	13 — 8
Information Centre	**i**
National Grid Reference	⁴05
Police Station	▲
Post Office	★
Safety Camera with Speed Limit Fixed cameras and long term road work cameras. Symbols do not indicate camera direction.	**30**
Toilet: without facilities for the Disabled with facilities for the Disabled	▽ ▽
Educational Establishment	▢
Hospital or Healthcare Building	▢
Industrial Building	▢
Leisure or Recreational Facility	▢
Place of Interest	▢
Public Building	▢
Shopping Centre or Market	▢
Other Selected Buildings	▢

SCALE

1:15,840
4 inches (10.16 cm) to 1 mile
6.31 cm to 1 km

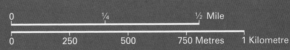

0 ¼ ½ Mile
0 250 500 750 Metres 1 Kilometre

A-Z A̶Z̶ AtoZ
registered trade marks of
Geographers' A-Z Map Company Ltd

www./az.co.uk

EDITION 4 2015
Copyright © Geographers' A-Z Map Co. Ltd.
Telephone: 01732 781000 (Enquiries & Trade Sales)
01732 783422 (Retail Sales)

© Crown copyright and database rights 2015 OS 100017302.

Safety camera information supplied by www.PocketGPSWorld.com.
Speed Camera Location Database Copyright 2015 © PocketGPSWorld.com

Every possible care has been taken to ensure that, to the best of our knowledge, the information contained in this atlas is accurate at the date of publication. However, we cannot warrant that our work is entirely error free and whilst we would be grateful to learn of any inaccuracies, we do not accept responsibility for loss or damage resulting from reliance on information contained within this publication.

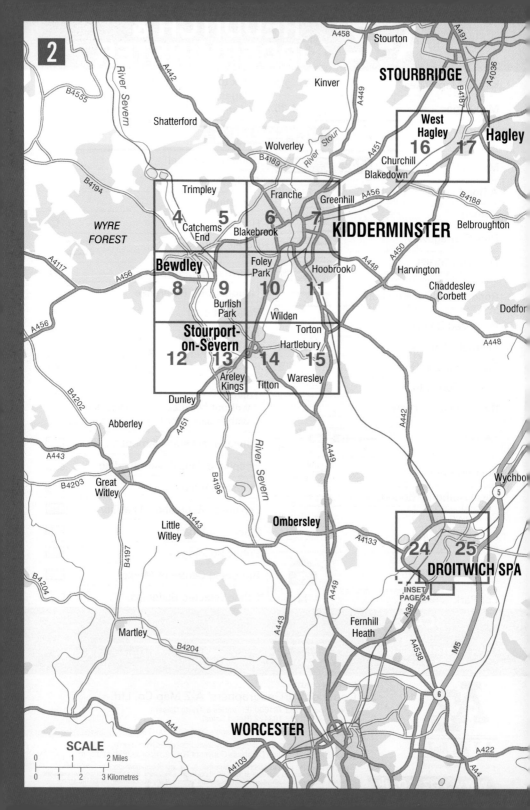

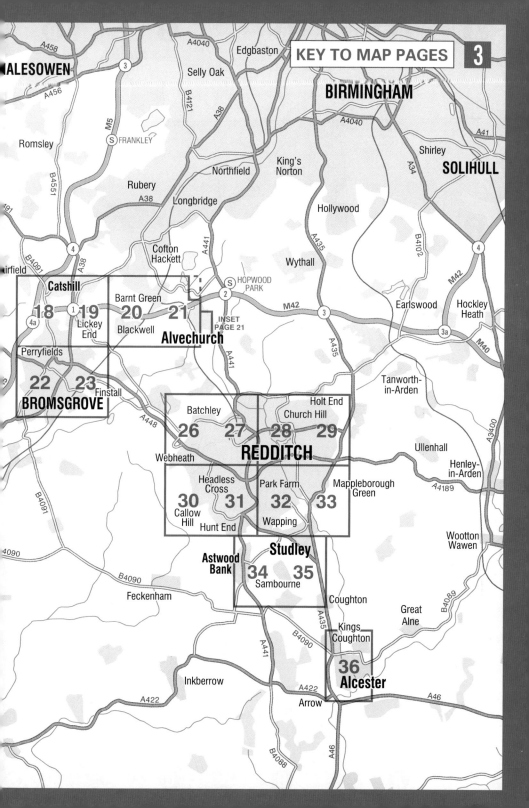

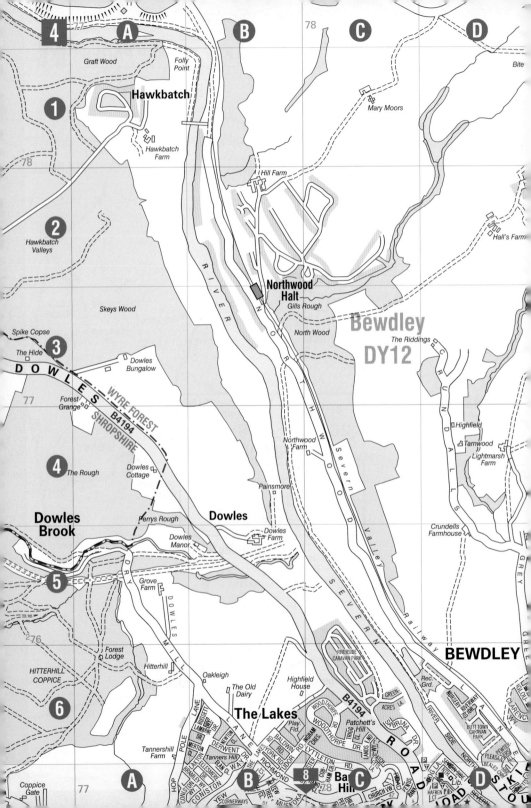

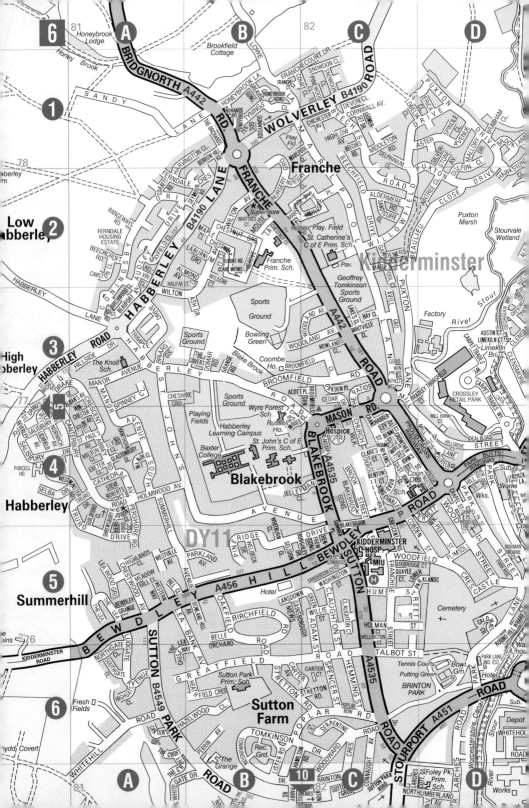

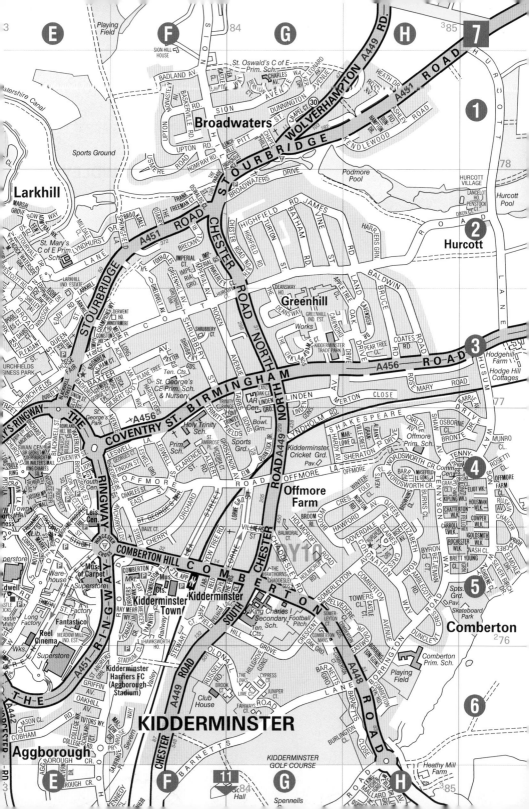

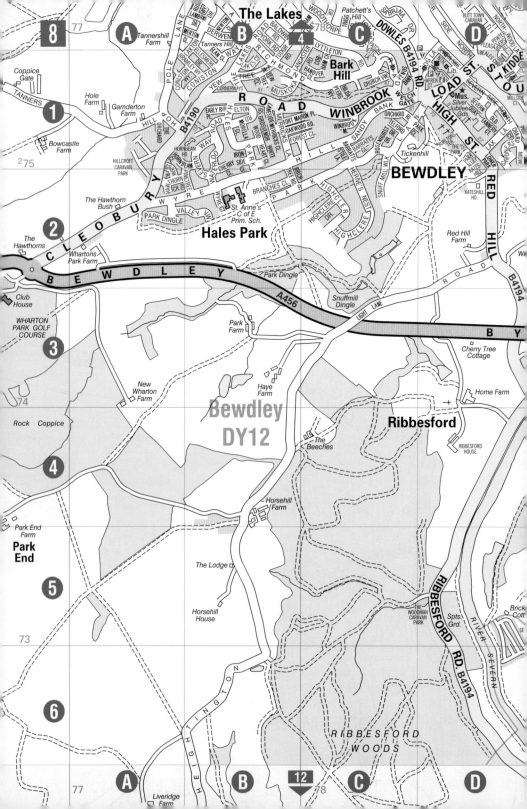

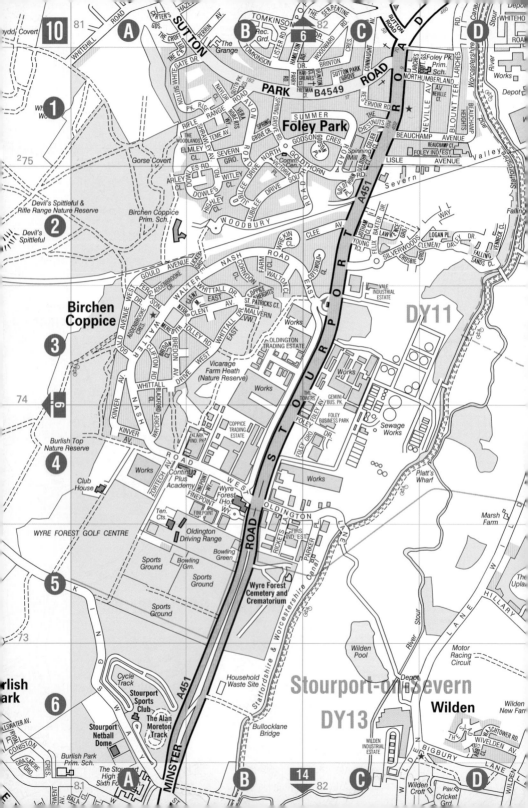

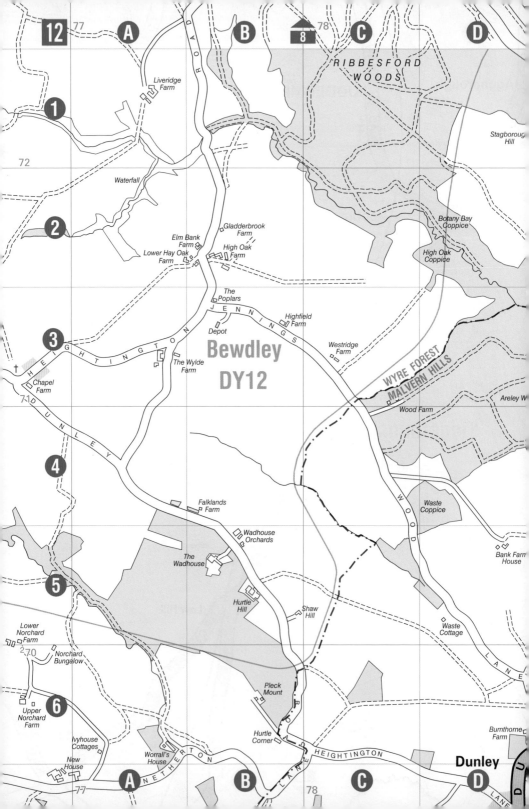

12 77 **A** **B** 8 78 **C** **D**

1

72

Liveridge Farm

2

Waterfall

RIBBESFORD WOODS

Stagborough Hill

Gladderbrook Farm

Elm Bank Farm

Lower Hay Oak Farm

High Oak Farm

Botany Bay Coppice

High Oak Coppice

The Poplars

Highfield Farm

Depot

Westridge Farm

Bewdley DY12

WYRE FOREST

MALVERN HILLS

3

The Wylde Farm

Chapel Farm

71

Wood Farm

Areley W

4

Falklands Farm

Wadhouse Orchards

The Wadhouse

Waste Coppice

5

Hurtle Hill

Shaw Hill

Bank Farm House

Lower Norchard Farm

Norchard Bungalow

Waste Cottage

270

6

Upper Norchard Farm

Pleck Mount

Ivyhouse Cottages

New House

Worrall's House

Hurtle Corner

Burnthorne Farm

Dunley

A 77 **B** 78 **C** **D**

HEIGHTINGTON

NETHERTON LANE

HEIGHTINGTON

DUNLEY

ROAD

JENNINGS

WOOD LANE

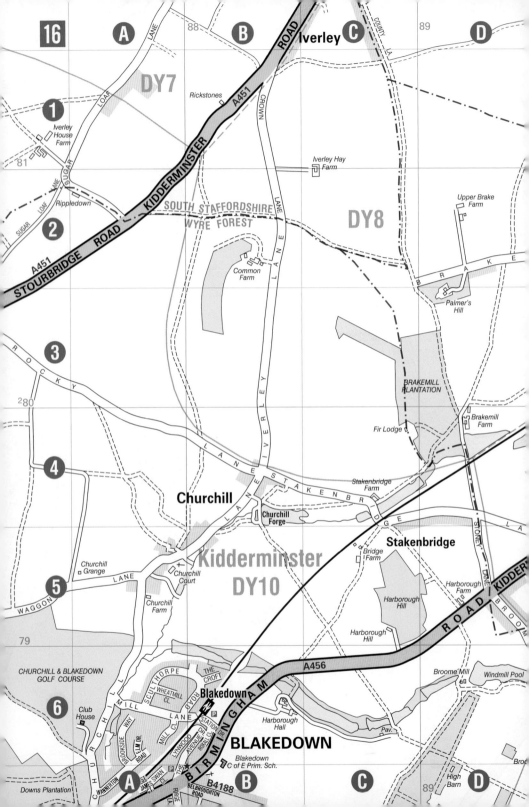

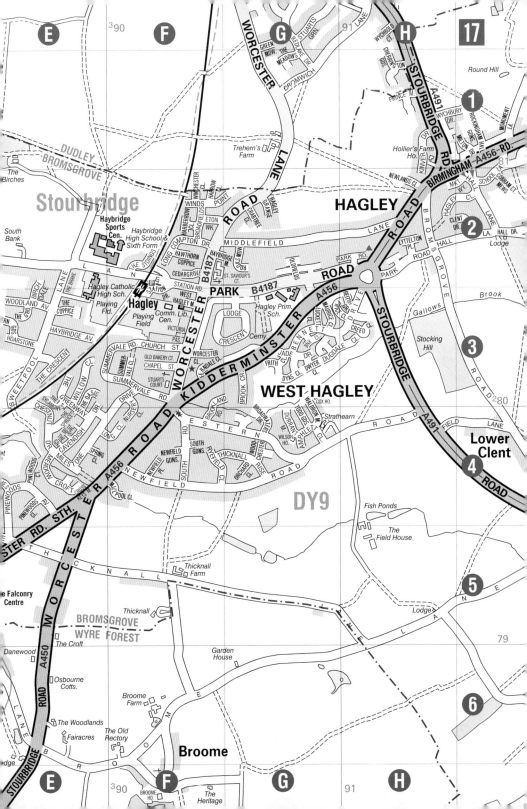

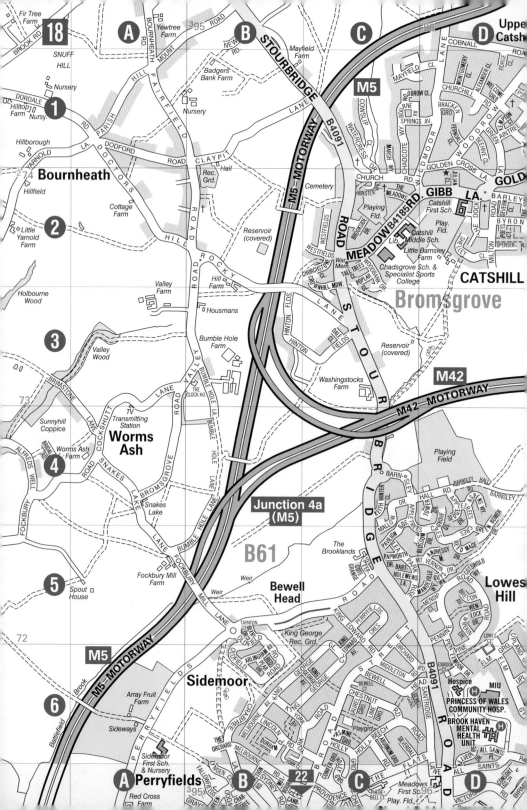

Grid references (top): E, F, G, H, 19

Grid references (bottom): E, F, 23, G, H

Places and areas:
- Lower Marlbrook
- Upper Marlbrook
- Lickey Rock
- Staple Hill
- Hall Flat
- Lickey End
- Little Heath
- Long Eye
- B60
- Burcot
- Green Hill
- Apes

Roads and routes:
- BIRMINGHAM ROAD (A38)
- B4096
- B4185
- OLD BIRMINGHAM ROAD
- LICKEY LANE
- LINEHOUSE LANE
- BROOKHOUSE LANE
- M42 MOTORWAY / M42-MOTORWAY
- SHEPLEY LANE
- SPIRE HOUSE LANE
- LEICESTER ROAD
- DALE LANE
- GREEN HILL
- BROMSGROVE EASTERN BY-PASS A38
- BURCOT LANE
- BLACKWELL ROAD
- PIKES POOL LA.
- HEATH ROAD
- Junction 1
- M42 Junction 1
- Junction 20

Other labels:
- Bellevue
- LivingWell Health Club
- Hotel
- CROSS LA.
- Rec. Grd. Pav.
- Greenfield Av.
- Hillside Farm
- Lickey Grange
- Firs Farm
- Firs Lodge
- The Grange
- Round Hill
- Nursery
- Gorse Hill
- Yewtree Farm
- Larks Hill
- Brookhouse
- North Bromsgrove Cemetery
- MARL-GROVE CT.
- Staple Farm
- TOPAZ WY.
- TOPAZ BUSINESS PARK
- Sand Pit
- Lower Shepley Farm
- The Beeches
- Upper Shepley Farm
- Astwood House
- Play. Fld.
- Lodge
- Hunter Techn. Co.
- Hillfield Farm
- Depot
- Nursery School
- HALL
- Club
- Nursery
- Little Heath Farm
- Wadderton
- The Uplands
- Crows Mill Farm
- Rec. Grd.
- SOUTH-MEAD DR.
- SCHOOL
- THE RETREAT
- THE TRYST
- GROSVENOR GDNS.
- Spadesbourne Brook
- Mill Pond
- Crows Mill
- Ashborough
- Cottage Farm
- Astwood Cottages
- Burcot Grange (Residential Home)
- Playing Fld.
- Infield
- Reservoir (covered)
- Depot
- Brooklands Farm
- Nursery
- Nursery
- Nursery
- Subway
- White House
- Hill Farm
- TOWNSEND AV.
- Spadesbourne Suite (Coun. Offs.)

Marker numbers: 1, 2, 3, 4, 5, 6, 19, 20, 23

Page number markers: 97, 98

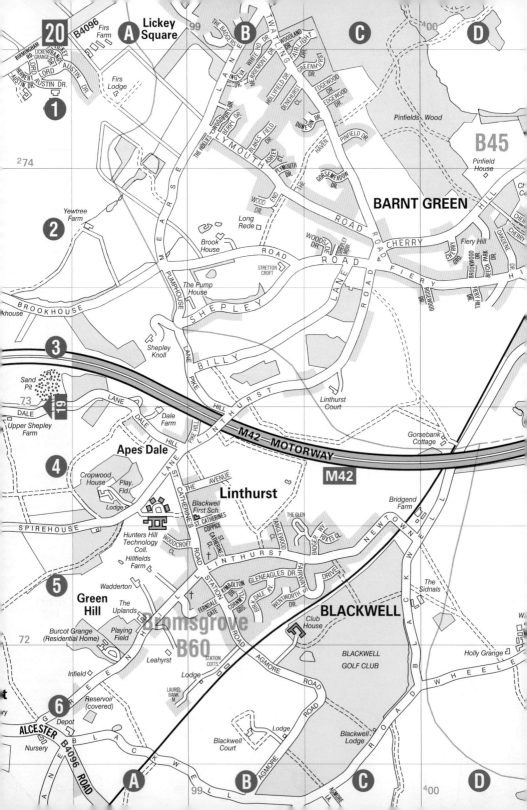

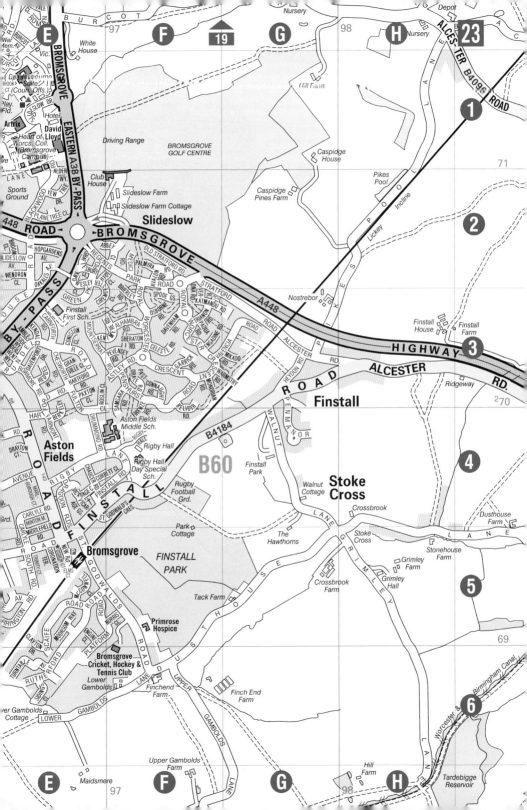

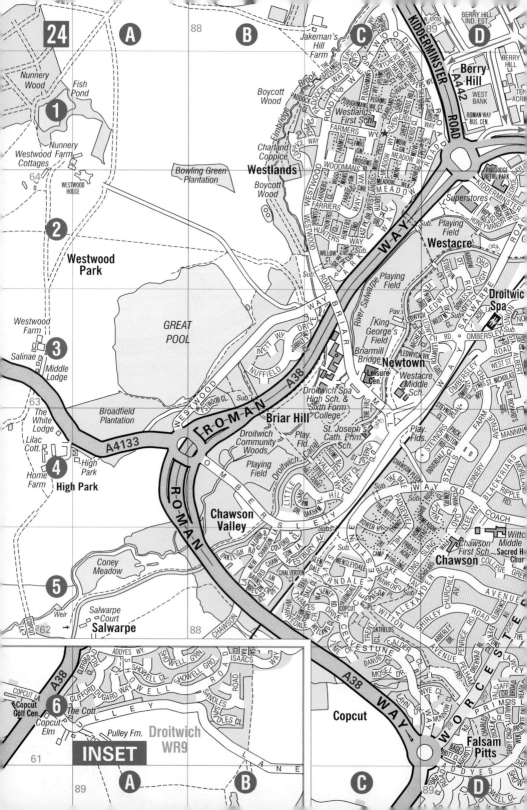

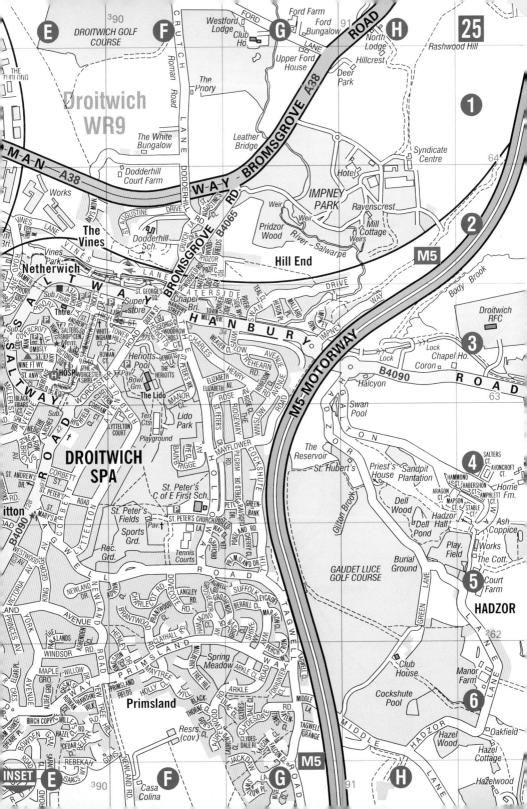

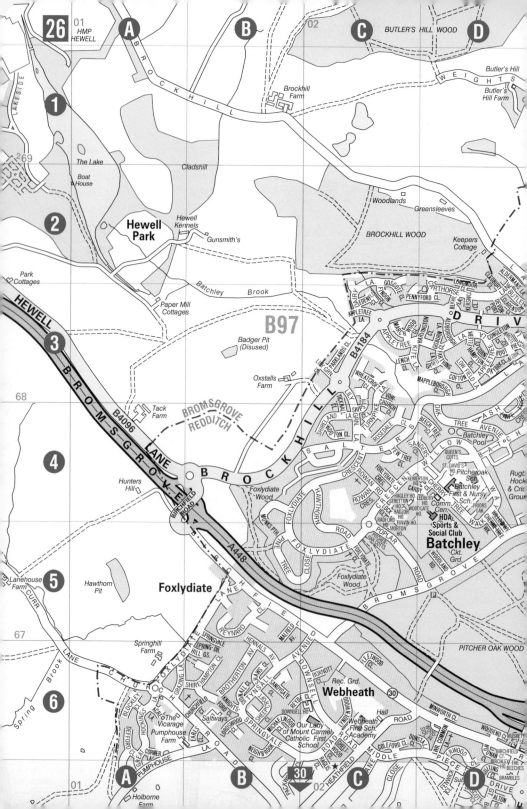

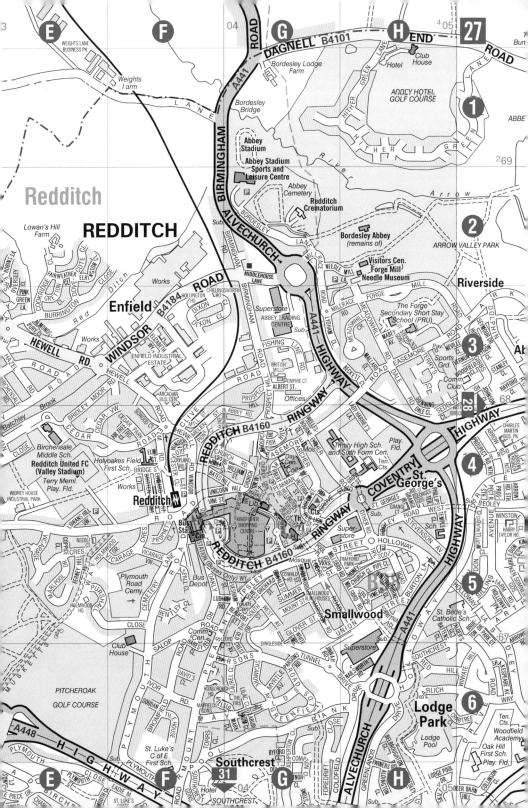

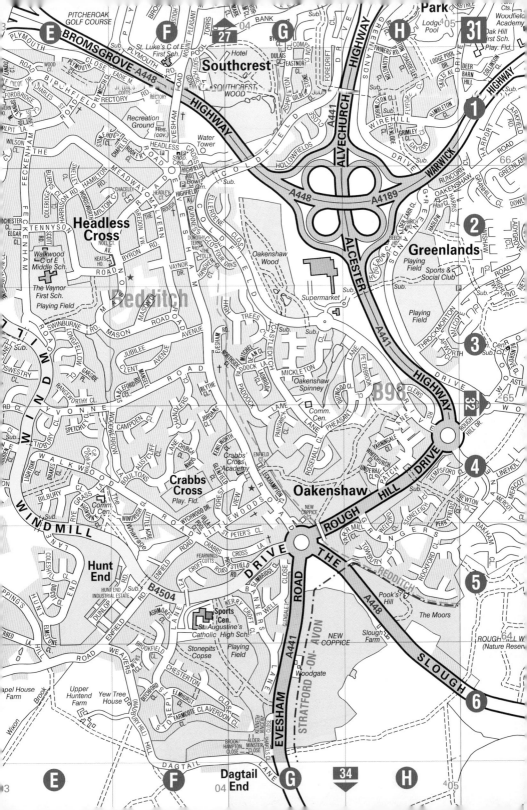

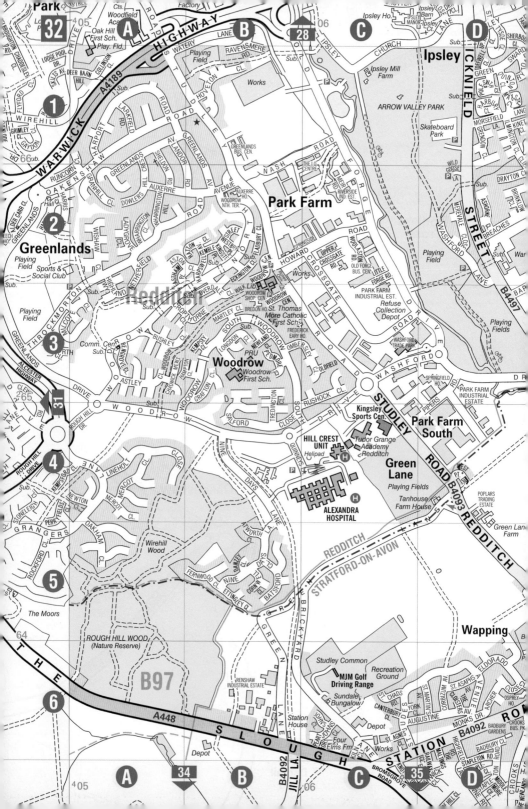

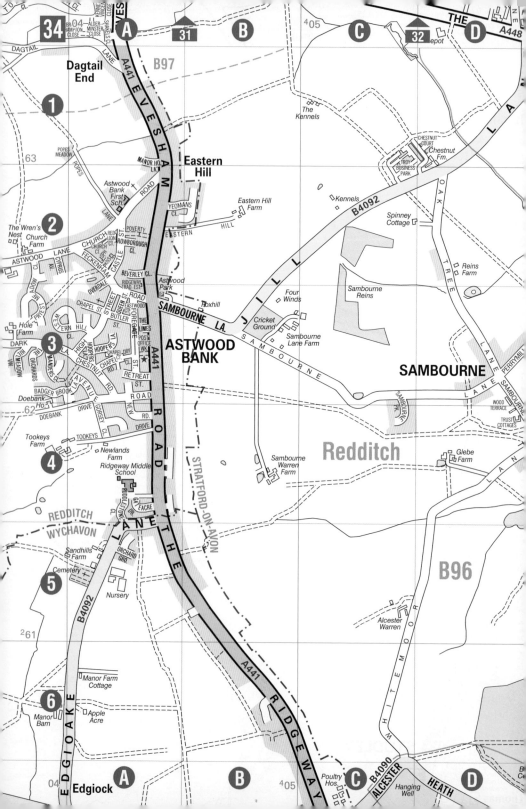

INDEX

Including Streets, Places & Areas, Hospitals etc., Industrial Estates, Selected Flats & Walkways, Junction Names & Service Areas, Stations and Selected Places of Interest.

HOW TO USE THIS INDEX

1. Each street name is followed by its Postcode District, then by its Locality abbreviation(s) and then by its map reference; e.g. **Abberley Av.** DY13: Stour S . . . .5F **13** is in the DY13 Postcode District and the Stourport-on-Severn Locality and is to be found in square 5F on page **13**. The page number is shown in bold type.
2. A strict alphabetical order is followed in which Av., Rd., St., etc. (though abbreviated) are read in full and as part of the street name; e.g. **Black Soils Rd.** appears after **Blacksmith Dr.** but before **Blackstitch La.**
3. Streets and a selection of flats and walkways that cannot be shown on the mapping, appear in the index with the thoroughfare to which they are connected shown in brackets; e.g. **Abberton Ho.** *B97: Redd . . . .4C **26** (off Lock Cl.)*
4. Addresses that are in more than one part are referred to as not continuous.
5. Places and areas are shown in the index in **BLUE TYPE** and the map reference is to the actual map square in which the town centre or area is located and not to the place name shown on the map; e.g. ALCESTER 5B 36
6. An example of a selected place of interest is **Avoncroft Mus. of Historic Buildings 6B 22**
7. Examples of stations are: **Alvechurch Station (Rail) . . . .6H 21; Bromsgrove Bus Station 2C 22**
8. Junction names and Service Areas are shown in the index in **BOLD CAPITAL TYPE**; e.g. **ARROW RDBT. 6A 36**
9. An example of a Hospital, Hospice or selected Healthcare facility is **ALEXANDRA HOSPITAL 4C 32**

GENERAL ABBREVIATIONS

All. : Alley
App. : Approach
Av. : Avenue
Bldgs. : Buildings
Bus. : Business
Cvn. : Caravan
Cen. : Centre
Chu. : Church
Cl. : Close
Comn. : Common
Cnr. : Corner
Cott. : Cottage
Cotts. : Cottages
Ct. : Court
Cres. : Crescent
Cft. : Croft
Dr. : Drive
E. : East
Ent. : Enterprise
Est. : Estate
Fld. : Field
Flds. : Fields
Gdn. : Garden
Gdns. : Gardens
Ga. : Gate
Gt. : Great
Grn. : Green
Gro. : Grove
Hgts. : Heights
Ho. : House
Ho's. : Houses
Ind. : Industrial
Info. : Information
La. : Lane
Lit. : Little
Lwr. : Lower
Mnr. : Manor
Mans. : Mansions
Mkt. : Market
Mdw. : Meadow
Mdws. : Meadows
M. : Mews
Mt. : Mount
Mus. : Museum
Nth. : North
No. : Number
Pk. : Park
Pas. : Passage
Pl. : Place
Pct. : Precinct
Ri. : Rise
Rd. : Road
Rdbt. : Roundabout
Shop. : Shopping
Sth. : South
Sq. : Square
Sta. : Station
St. : Street
Ter. : Terrace
Trad. : Trading
Up. : Upper
Va. : Vale
Vw. : View
Vis. : Visitors
Wlk. : Walk
W. : West
Yd. : Yard

LOCALITY ABBREVIATIONS

Alc : **Alcester**
A'chu : **Alvechurch**
Arr : **Arrow**
A'wd B : **Astwood Bank**
Bks G : **Banks Green**
B Grn : **Barnt Green**
Beo : **Beoley**
Bew : **Bewdley**
B'wll : **Blackwell**
Blak : **Blakedown**
Bourn : **Bournheath**
B'gve : **Bromsgrove**
Brme : **Broome**
Burc : **Burcot**
Cats : **Catshill**
C'wick : **Chadwick**
C'hll : **Churchill**
Clent : **Clent**
Coft H : **Cofton Hackett**
Cop : **Copcut**
Cou : **Coughton**
C'way G : **Crossway Green**
D'frd : **Dodford**
Droit S : **Droitwich Spa**
Dunl : **Dunley**
Elc B : **Elcock's Brook**
Elmb : **Elmbridge**
F'fld : **Fairfield**
Fins : **Finstall**
Had : **Hadzor**
Hag : **Hagley**
Ham G : **Ham Green**
H Lov : **Hampton Lovett**
Hartl : **Hartlebury**
Heigh : **Heightington**
Hurc : **Hurcott**
Ism : **Ismere**
I'ley : **Iverley**
Kidd : **Kidderminster**
King C : **King's Coughton**
Kinw : **Kinwarton**
Lick : **Lickey**
Lick E : **Lickey End**
Low H : **Low Habberley**
Map G : **Mappleborough Green**
Marlb : **Marlbrook**
Newl : **Newland**
Ove G : **Oversley Green**
Pedm : **Pedmore**
Rash : **Rashwood**
Redd : **Redditch**
Ribb : **Ribbesford**
Salw : **Salwarpe**
Sam : **Sambourne**
Shens : **Shenstone**
Sper : **Spernal**
Stoke H : **Stoke Heath**
Stoke P : **Stoke Pound**
S Prior : **Stoke Prior**
Stone : **Stone**
Stour S : **Stourport-on-Severn**
Stud : **Studley**
Tard : **Tardebigge**
Titt : **Titton**
Tort : **Torton**
Trim : **Trimpley**
Tutn : **Tutnall**
Up Ben : **Upper Bentley**
U War : **Upton Warren**
Ware : **Waresley**
Westw : **Westwood**
Wild : **Wildmoor**
W'ley : **Wolverley**

I O Centre, The B98: Redd 1C **32**

A

Abberley Av. DY13: Stour S 5F **13**
Abberley Cl. B98: Redd 3C **28**
Abberley Dr. WR9: Droit S 5D **24**
Abberton Ho. *B97: Redd . . . . 4C **26** (off Lock Cl.)*
Abbey Cl. B49: Alc 3A **36**
B60: B'gve 2F **23**
ABBEYDALE 3A 28
Abbeyfields Dr. B80: Stud 4E **33**
Abbey Hotel Golf Course 1H **27**
Abbey M. B49: Alc 5B **36**
Abbey Rd. B97: Redd 4G **27**
DY11: Kidd 4A **6**
Abbey Stadium 1G **27**
Abbey Stadium Sports & Leisure Cen. 1G **27**
Abbey Trad. Cen. B97: Redd 3G **27**
Abbotswood Cl. B98: Redd 5G **29**
Abbotts Cl. DY13: Stour S 6D **10**
Acacia Av. DY12: Bew 1E **9**
Acanthus Rd. B98: Redd 2F **29**
Acorn Ent. Cen. DY11: Kidd 3F **11**
Acorn Rd. B61: Cats 1E **19**
Acorns, The B61: Cats 2D **18**
Acre La. B97: Redd 6A **26**
WR9: Droit S 3D **24**
Acton Cl. B98: Redd 3D **28**
Adams Ct. DY10: Kidd 3G **7**
Adams Ho. DY11: Kidd 4C **6**
Adam St. DY11: Kidd 5C **6**
Adams Way B49: Alc 3B **36**
Addenbrooke Cres. DY11: Kidd . . . . 3A **10** (not continuous)
Addenbrooke Rd. WR9: Droit S 4E **25**
Addyes Grn. WR9: Droit S 6D **24**
Addyes Way WR9: Droit S 6A **24**
Adelaide St. B97: Redd 4F **27**
Admiral Wlk. DY10: Kidd 2E **7**
Adrian Cl. WR9: Droit S 5F **25**
AGGBOROUGH 6E 7
Aggborough Cres. DY10: Kidd 1E **11**
Aggborough Stadium 6F **7**
Agmore La. B60: Tard 6C **20**
Agmore Rd. B60: B'wll 6B **20**
Aintree Cl. B61: Cats 1D **18**
DY11: Kidd 2D **6**
Alan Moreton Track, The 6A **10**
Alauna Av. B49: Alc 3C **36**
Albany Cl. DY10: Kidd 4H **7**
Albert Cl. B80: Stud 6E **33**
Albert Ho. B98: Redd 2C **28**
Albert Rd. B61: B'gve 4B **22**
DY10: Kidd 4F **7**
Albert St. B97: Redd 3G **27**
WR9: Droit S 3D **24**
Albury Rd. B80: Stud 6E **33**
ALCESTER 5B 36
Alcester Heath B49: Alc 6C **34**
B49: King C 2A **36**
Alcester Highway B98: Redd 2H **31**
Alcester Rd. B60: Burc, Lick E 4F **19**
B60: Fins, Tard, Tutn 3G **23**
B80: Stud 6E **33**
B98: Beo 3H **29**
Alcester St. B97: Redd 5G **27**
B98: Redd 4G **27**
Alcester Wlk. *B97: Redd . . . . 4G **27** (off Kingfisher Shop. Cen.)*
Alcocks Rd. B49: Alc 4D **36**
Aldborough La. B97: Redd 3D **26**
Alder Av. DY10: Kidd 2D **6**
Alderbrook Cl. B97: Redd 3D **26**
Alderbrook Rd. WR9: Droit S 5B **24**
Alder Carr Cl. B98: Redd 2H **31**
Alder Gro. WR9: Droit S 6E **25**
Alderley Rd. B61: B'gve 4A **22**
Aldermans La. B97: Redd 2D **26**
Aldermere Rd. DY11: Kidd 2C **6**
Alderminster Cl. B97: Redd 6G **31**
Alder's Cl. B98: Redd 5A **28**
Alders Dr. B98: Redd 4F **29**
Alder Way B60: B'gve 2E **23**
Aldington Cl. B98: Redd 1H **31**
Alexander Av. WR9: Droit S 5C **24**
Alexander Cl. B61: Cats 1D **18**
ALEXANDRA HOSPITAL 4C **32**
Alfreds Well B61: D'frd 4A **18**
Alhambra Rd. B60: B'gve 3F **23**
Allen Cl. B80: Stud 2G **35**
Allendale Av. B80: Stud 1G **35**
Allendale Ct. B80: Stud 1G **35**
Allendale Cres. B80: Stud 1G **35**
Allensmore Cl. B98: Redd 6F **29**
Allimore La. B49: Alc 4A **36**
All Saints Av. DY12: Bew 6E **5**
All Saints Pl. B61: B'gve 6D **18**
All Saints Rd. B61: B'gve 1D **22**
Allwoods Cl. B49: Alc 4A **36**
Almond Av. DY11: Kidd 2B **6**
Almondsbury Cl. B97: Redd 3E **27**
Almond Way DY13: Stour S 1F **13**
Alne Bank Rd. B49: Alc 4D **36**
Althestan Cl. B48: A'chu 3H **21**
Alton Cl. B97: Redd 1D **30**
ALVECHURCH 1H 21
Alvechurch Highway B97: Redd 2G **27**
B98: Redd 2G **27**
Alvechurch Ho. *B60: B'gve . . . . 1E **23** (off Burcot La.)*
Alvechurch Station (Rail) 6H 21
Alveley Cl. B98: Redd 4D **28**
Alveston Cl. B98: Redd 6C **28**
Ambergate Cl. B97: Redd 3D **26**
Amblecote Rd. DY10: Kidd 5H **7**
Ambleside Way B60: B'gve 3E **23**
Amelia Ter. DY13: Stour S 3B **14**
Amphlett Cl. DY9: Hag 4G **17**
Amphlett Ct. B60: B'gve 2D **22**
WR9: Had 4H **25**
Anchor Dr. DY13: Stour S 3B **14**
Anchorfields DY10: Kidd 4F **7**
Andressy M. B61: B'gve 5D **18**
Ankerdine Av. *DY13: Stour S . . . . 5F **13** (off Langdale Rd.)*
Ansley Cl. B98: Redd 1F **33**
Anton Cl. DY12: Bew 5F **5**
APES DALE 4A 20
Apple Tree Cl. DY10: Kidd 2G **7**
Appletree La. B97: Redd 3C **26**
Appletrees Cres. B61: B'gve 4C **18**
Aqueduct La. B48: A'chu 3G **21**
Aragon Ct. WR9: Had 4H **25**
Arcadian Bus. Cen. B97: Redd 3F **27**
Archer Cl. B80: Stud 6D **32**

Archer Rd. B98: Redd 4G 27
Archers Cl. WR9: Droit S 3C 24
Arch Hill DY10: Kidd 4E 7
Arden Bus. Cen. B49: Alc 2B 36
Arden Ct. B49: Alc 2B 36
Arden Forest Ind. Est. B49: Kinw 2C 36
Arden Ho. B60: B'gve 1E 23
                                        (off Burcot La.)
Arden Rd. B49: Alc 3A 36
Ardens Cl. B98: Redd 6G 29
ARELEY COMMON 4G 13
Areley Comn. DY13: Stour S 6G 13
Areley Cl. DY13: Stour S 4F 13
ARELEY KINGS 5G 13
Areley La. DY13: Stour S 3F 13
Arkle Cl. WR9: Droit S 6G 25
Arkle Rd. WR9: Droit S 6G 25
Arley Cl. B98: Redd 3D 28
  DY11: Kidd .2A 10
Arlingham Av. B61: B'gve 6B 18
Arlington Ct. DY12: Bew 5E 5
Arran Cl. DY13: Stour S 3A 14
ARROW 6A 36
Arrow Cl. B49: Alc 3B 36
Arrow Cres. B49: Alc 3B 36
Arrow Cft. WR9: Droit S 2D 24
Arrowdale Rd. B98: Redd 5A 28
Arrow Rd. B98: Redd 4A 28
Arrow Rd. Nth. B98: Redd 4A 28
Arrow Rd. Sth. B98: Redd 4A 28
ARROW RDBT. 6A 36
Arrow Vale Sports Cen. 6E 29
Arrow Valley Country Pk. 4B 28
Arrow Valley Vis. Cen. 4C 28
Arrow Vw. B80: Stud 5E 33
Arthur Dr. DY11: Kidd 3E 11
Arthur Jobson Ho. B98: Redd 4A 28
Arthur St. B98: Redd 5A 28
Arthur St. Cen. B98: Redd 5A 28
Artrix 1E 23
Arundel Rd. B60: B'gve 2D 22
Ascot Way B61: Cats 1E 19
Ashdene Cl. DY10: Kidd 5H 7
  DY11: Hartl .4G 15
Ash Dr. B61: Cats 1D 18
Ashenden Cl. WR9: Droit S 5E 25
Ash Gro. DY11: Kidd 3B 6
  DY13: Stour S 2G 13
Ashgrove Cl. B60: Marlb 1G 19
Ashley Rd. DY10: Kidd 1H 7
Ashmores Cl. B97: Redd 5F 31
Ashorne Cl. B98: Redd 2D 32
Ashperton Cl. B98: Redd 1G 31
Ashton Cl. B97: Redd 1D 30
Ash Tree Rd. B97: Redd 4D 26
Aspall Cl. B97: Redd 5F 27
Aspen Cl. B49: Alc 3B 36
Aspens Way B61: B'gve 4D 18
Aspen Wlk. DY13: Stour S 1G 13
Aster Av. DY11: Kidd 1D 6
Astley Cl. B98: Redd 3A 32
Astley Ct. DY13: Stour S 6G 13
ASTLEY CROSS 6G 13
Astley Rd. B60: B'gve 3F 23
Aston Cl. B98: Redd 2A 32
Aston Ct. B60: B'gve 6D 22
ASTON FIELDS 5D 22
Aston Flds. Trad. Est. B60: B'gve 6C 22
Aston Rd. B60: B'gve 6C 22
ASTWOOD BANK 3A 34
Astwood La. B96: A'wd B 2A 34
Atcham Cl. B98: Redd 5F 29
Atcheson Cl. B80: Stud 6E 33
Atherstone Cl. B98: Redd 1F 33
Atworth Cl. B98: Redd 5B 32
Audley Dr. DY11: Kidd 2A 6
Augustine Av. B80: Stud 6D 32
Augustus Dr. B49: Alc 5B 36
Austcliff Cl. B97: Redd 4F 31
Austin Ct. DY10: Kidd 3D 6
Austin Rd. B60: B'gve 5B 22
Auxerre Av. B98: Redd 2A 32
Auxerre Ho. B98: Redd 2B 32
Avalon Rd. B60: B'gve 2F 23
Avenbury Cl. B98: Redd 1F 33
Avenue, The B60: B'wll 6A 16
  DY10: Blak .6A 16
  DY11: Kidd .4G 11
  DY11: Ware .6G 15
Avenue Rd. B96: A'wd B 3A 34
Avill Gro. DY11: Kidd 3C 6
Avocet Dr. DY10: Kidd 2G 11
Avonbank Cl. B97: Redd 4E 31
Avon Cl. B60: B'gve 6C 22
Avon Cres. B49: Alc 3C 36
Avoncroft Ct. WR9: Had 4H 25
Avoncroft Mus. of Historic Buildings . . .6B 22
Avoncroft Rd. B60: Stoke H 6A 22
Avondale Rd. WR9: Droit S 5C 24
Avon Rd. DY11: Kidd 1B 10

B

Badbury Cl. B80: Stud 6D 32
Badbury Gdns. B80: Stud 6D 32

Badger Brook La. B96: A'wd B 3A 34
Badger Cl. B98: Redd 5D 28
Badgers, The B45: B Grn 1B 20
Badgers Wlk. DY13: Stour S 2H 13
Badger Way B60: B'wll 5C 20
Badland Av. DY10: Kidd 1F 7
Bagehott Cl. WR9: Droit S 6D 24
Bagehott Rd. WR9: Droit S 6D 24
Bainbrigge Av. WR9: Droit S 4F 25
Baize Ct. DY10: Kidd 5F 7
Bala Cl. DY13: Stour S 1A 14
Baldwin Gdns. DY13: Stour S 2B 14
Baldwin Rd. DY10: Kidd 2H 7
  DY12: Bew .6B 4
  DY13: Stour S 2B 14
Balmoral Ct. DY10: Kidd 5G 7
Bank Ho. B96: A'wd B 3A 34
                                        (off Evesham Rd.)
Banners La. B97: Redd 5G 31
Bant Mill Rd. B60: B'gve 3D 22
Barford Cl. B98: Redd 1F 33
BARK HILL 1C 8
Barley Cft. B60: Stoke H 5A 22
Barley Mow La. B61: Cats 2D 18
Barlich Way B98: Redd 6H 27
Barlichway B49: Alc 4D 36
Barn Cl. B60: Stoke H 6B 22
Barnetts Cl. DY10: Kidd 6H 7
Barnetts Gro. DY10: Kidd 6G 7
Barnetts La. DY10: Kidd 1F 11
Barnfield Rd. B61: B'gve 3B 22
Barn Owl Pl. DY10: Kidd 2G 11
Barns Cft. Way WR9: Droit S 5B 24
Barnsley Hall Dr. B61: B'gve, Lick E . . .4D 18
Barnsley Hall Rd. B61: B'gve, Lick E . . .4C 18
Barnsley Rd. B61: B'gve 6E 19
BARNT GREEN 2E 21
Barnt Green Station (Rail) 2E 21
Barnwood Rd. B98: Redd 3D 28
Barracks Rd. DY13: Stour S 5C 14
Barratts Cl. DY12: Bew 1C 8
Barratts Stile La. DY12: Bew 1C 8
Barrett Cl. DY10: Kidd 4H 7
Barrie Av. DY10: Kidd 3H 7
Barrow Cl. B98: Redd 5F 29
Bartestree Cl. B98: Redd 1F 33
Bartholemews La. B61: B'gve 5C 18
Bartleet Rd. B98: Redd 3D 32
Bascote Cl. B97: Redd 1D 30
Basepoint B60: B'gve 6D 22
Baskerville Rd. DY10: Kidd 1F 7
BATCHLEY 4D 26
Batchley Rd. B97: Redd 4D 26
Bates Hill B97: Redd 4F 27
Batham Rd. DY10: Kidd 2G 7
Batsford Cl. B98: Redd 5B 32
Battens Cl. B98: Redd 5H 27
Battens Dr. B98: Redd 4D 28
Baxter Av. DY10: Kidd 3E 7
Baxter Gdns. DY10: Kidd 3F 7
Bays Mdw. WR9: Droit S 2E 25
Beach Rd. DY13: Stour S 5G 13
Beacon Cl. B49: Alc 3C 36
Beales Cnr. DY12: Bew 1D 8
Bear Hill B48: A'chu 2H 21
Bear Hill Dr. B48: A'chu 1H 21
Beauchamp Av. DY11: Kidd 1C 10
Beauchamp Ct. B49: King C 2A 36
  DY11: Kidd .1D 10
Beauchamp Hgts. DY11: Kidd 1D 10
Beaufort Av. DY11: Kidd 3A 6
Beaufort St. B98: Redd 5G 27
Beaulieu Cl. DY11: Kidd 2C 6
Beaulieu Ho. DY13: Stour S 3A 14
Beaumont Lawns B60: Marlb 1F 19
Beckett Cl. B98: Redd 3H 27
Becks, The B48: A'chu 3H 21
Beech Cl. B49: Ove G 6D 36
Beechcroft Dr. B61: B'gve 6E 19
Beechcroft Rd. DY11: Kidd 2A 6
Beeches, The B97: Redd 1D 30
Beeches M. DY9: Hag 4E 17
Beeches Rd. DY11: Kidd 1C 6
Beechfield Dr. DY11: Kidd 1C 6
Beech Ho. B98: Redd 2H 31
Beech Pk. Dr. B45: B Grn 2G 21
Beech Rd. B61: B'gve 6C 18
Beech Tree Cl. B97: Redd 4D 26
Beehive Cl. B61: Cats 1D 18
Belbroughton Cl. B98: Redd 6H 27
Belbroughton Rd. DY10: Blak 6B 16
Belfry Rd. WR9: Droit S 6E 25
Belle Orchard DY11: Kidd 5B 6
Belle Vue Cl. B61: Marlb 1F 19
Bell La. B80: Stud 6E 33
Bell Mead B80: Stud 6E 33
Bell Row DY13: Stour S 3A 14
                                        (off Lion Hill)
Belmont Cl. B97: Redd 1D 30
Belvedere Cl. DY10: Kidd 5G 7
Belvedere Cres. DY12: Bew 5E 5
Belvedere Dr. B61: B'gve 6D 18
Belvoir Rd. B60: B'gve 3F 23
Bengrove Cl. B98: Redd 3A 32
Bennett Dr. DY9: Hag 3G 17

Bennett St. DY11: Kidd 4C 6
Bentley Cl. B97: Redd 5F 27
Bentons Ct. DY11: Kidd 4C 6
BEOLEY 1D 28
Beoley La. B98: Beo 1E 29
Beoley Rd. E. B98: Redd 4A 28
Beoley Rd. W. B98: Redd 5H 27
Berkeley Cl. B60: B'gve 4E 23
  B98: Redd 5G 29
Berkeley Cres. DY13: Stour S 6A 14
Berkeswell Cl. B98: Redd 1B 28
Bernie Crossland Wlk. DY10: Kidd 1F 11
Berrill Cl. WR9: Droit S 5G 25
Berrington Cl. B98: Redd 6C 28
Berrow Hill Rd. DY11: Kidd 1B 6
Berrow Vw. B61: B'gve 2B 22
Berry Dr. B45: B Grn 1B 20
BERRY HILL .1D 24
Berry Hill WR9: Droit S 1D 24
Berry Hill Ind. Est. WR9: Droit S 1D 24
Betjeman Cl. DY10: Kidd 5H 7
Beverley Cl. B96: A'wd B 2A 34
  DY11: Kidd .4H 5
Beverley Ct. DY13: Stour S 2H 13
BEWDLEY 1D 8
Bewdley By-Pass DY12: Bew, Ribb 2A 8
Bewdley Grange DY11: Kidd 5A 6
Bewdley Hill DY11: Kidd 5A 6
Bewdley Leisure Cen. 2E 9
Bewdley Mus. 1D 8
Bewdley Pines Golf Course 4G 5
Bewdley Rd. DY11: Kidd 5C 6
  DY13: Stour S 1H 13
Bewdley Rd. Nth. DY13: Stour S 5F 9
Bewdley Station
  Severn Valley Railway 1E 9
Bewell Ct. B61: B'gve 6C 18
Bewell Gdns. B61: B'gve 6C 18
BEWELL HEAD 6C 18
Bewell Head B61: B'gve 6C 18
Bigbury La. DY13: Stour S 6D 10
Bilberry Cl. DY13: Stour S 1G 13
Bilbury Cl. B97: Redd 4E 31
Billy La. B45: B Grn 3B 20
  B60: B'wll 3B 20
Binton Cl. B98: Redd 1F 33
Birch Abbey B49: Alc 5B 36
Birch Coppice WR9: Droit S 6E 25
Birch Dale DY8: Hag 3E 17
BIRCHEN COPPICE 3A 10
Birchensale Rd. B97: Redd 3E 27
Birches, The DY11: Hartl 4H 15
  DY13: Stour S 3B 14
Birches La. B48: A'chu 4G 21
Birchfield Cl. B97: Redd 5A 28
Birchfield Dr. DY13: Stour S 1G 13
Birchfield Rd. B97: Redd 5A 28
  DY11: Kidd .5B 6
Birch Ho. B98: Redd 2H 31
Birchley Ho. B97: Redd 6D 26
Birch Tree Rd. DY12: Bew 2B 8
Birchwood Cl. DY11: Kidd 3A 6
Birkdale Av. B60: B'wll 6E 23
Birlingham Ho. B60: B'gve 1E 23
                                        (off Burcot La.)
Birmingham Rd. B48: A'chu . . . . .1H 21 & 3H 21
  B49: Alc 3A 36
  B49: Cou 6H 35
  B49: King C .1A 36
  B61: B'gve, Lick E, Marlb 1D 22
                                        (not continuous)
  B80: Map G, Stud 5E 33
  B97: Redd 2F 27
                                        (not continuous)
  DY9: Hag 2H 17
  DY10: Blak, Kidd 6B 16
Biset Av. DY10: Kidd 5H 7
Bishop Hall Cres. B60: B'gve 5B 22
Bishopstone Cl. B98: Redd 6F 29
Bishop St. DY13: Stour S 1A 14
Bittell Farm Rd. B45: B Grn 1G 21
Bittell La. B45: B Grn 2F 21
Bittell Rd. B45: B Grn 2E 21
Bittern Wood Rd. DY10: Kidd 1H 11
Blackford Cl. DY11: Kidd 3A 10
Blackfriars Av. WR9: Droit S 4D 24
Blackfriars Ct. WR9: Droit S 3E 25
Black Horse La. DY10: Kidd 4D 6
Blackmore La. B60: B'gve 3C 22
Blacksmith Dr. B60: B'gve 5D 22
Black Soils Rd. B98: Redd 3F 29
Blackstitch La. B97: Redd 1C 30
BLACKSTONE 3F 9
Blackstone DY12: Bew 5E 9
Blackstone Riverside Pk. 3E 9
Blackthorn Ct. B98: Redd 1E 33
Blackthorne Cl. WR9: Droit S 6F 25
Blackthorn Way B49: Alc 3B 36
BLACKWELL .5C 20
Blackwell Golf Club 5G 20
Blackwell La. B97: Redd 3D 26
Blackwell Rd. B45: B Grn 5C 20
  B60: B'wll 6A 20
Blackwell St. DY10: Kidd 4E 7
Blackwood Rd. B60: B'gve 2E 23
Blake Av. WR9: Droit S 5C 24
BLAKEBROOK 4C 6

Blakebrook DY11: Kidd .4C 6
(not continuous)
Blakebrook Cl. DY11: Kidd 4C 6
Blakebrook Gdns. DY11: Kidd 4C 6
BLAKEDOWN 6A 16
Blakedown Station (Rail) 6B 16
Blakemere Cl. D90: Redd 5F 29
Blakeney Dr. B61: B'gve 5B 18
Blake Rd. B61: Cats 2E 19
Blakes Fld. Dr. B45: B Grn 1B 20
Blaze La. B97: Redd 6D 30
Bleachfield St. B49: Alc 1D 42
Blenheim Cres. B60: B'gve 4D 22
Blockley Cl. B97: Redd 6A 26
Blossom Cl. B61: B'gve 5D 18
Blount Ho. DY11: Kidd 2B 6
Blount Ter. DY11: Kidd 1D 10
Blythe Cl. B97: Redd 3F 31
Blythesway B48: A'chu 4H 21
Bodenham Cl. B98: Redd 5D 28
Boehm Dr. B49: Kinw .3D 36
Booton Ct. DY10: Kidd 1G 7
Boot Piece La. B97: Redd 3D 26
Bordesley Abbey 2H 27
Bordesley Abbey Vis. Cen. 2H 27
Bordesley La. B97: Redd 2G 27
Borrington Gdns. DY10: Kidd 6H 7
Borrington Rd. DY10: Kidd 6H 7
Boteler Cl. B49: Alc 5B 36
Boultons La. B97: Redd 6F 27
Bourne Av. B61: Cats .1C 18
Bourne Cl. WR9: Droit S 3E 25
BOURNHEATH 1A 18
Bournheath Rd. B61: F'fld 1A 18
Bowden Grn. WR9: Droit S 6E 25
Bower Bank DY13: Stour S 4G 13
Bower Hill WR9: Droit S 4C 24
Bower Hill Dr. DY13: Stour S 4G 13
Bowmore Rd. B60: B'gve 3E 23
Bowood Ct. B97: Redd 4F 27
Bowpatch Cl. DY13: Stour S 5F 13
Bowpatch Rd. DY13: Stour S 5F 13
Boxnott Cl. B97: Redd 6C 26
Brabham Cl. DY11: Kidd 1D 6
Braces La. B60: Marlb 1E 19
Bracken Gro. B61: Cats 1D 18
Bradley Thursfield Ct. DY11: Kidd 3C 6
Braeburn Cl. DY13: Stour S 1G 13
Brake, The DY8: Hag 2E 17
Brake La. DY8: Hag 2D 16
Bramble Ho. B98: Redd 2H 3
(off Alder Carr Cl.)
Brambles B97: Redd 1D 30
Brambles, The B61: Cats 2D 18
Brambling Ri. DY10: Kidd 3H 11
Bramley Way DY12: Bew 1A 8
Branches Cl. DY12: Bew 4E 9
Brant Farm Cvn. Site DY12: Bew 4E 9
Brantwood Cl. WR9: Droit S 5F 25
Brantwood Rd. WR9: Droit S 5F 25
Breaches La. B98: Redd 2D 32
Breakback Rd. B61: B'gve 4A 22
Brecknell Ri. DY10: Kidd 2F 7
Brecon Av. B61: B'gve 5D 18
Brecon Cl. WR9: Droit S 5B 24
Bredon Av. DY11: Kidd 3A 10
Bredon Cl. DY11: Kidd 3A 10
Bredon Ho. B98: Redd 3B 32
Bredon Rd. B61: B'gve 5A 22
Bredon Vw. B97: Redd 2F 31
Bredon Way DY13: Stour S 5F 13
Breedon Gdns. B98: Redd 5A 28
Breme Lodge B60: B'gve 5D 22
Brett Young Cl. DY10: Kidd 5H 7
Briar Cl. B60: Lick E 4F 19
BRIAR HILL 4B 24
Briar Mill WR9: Droit S 3C 24
Briars, The DY9: Hag .4E 17
Briars Gdns. DY11: Kidd 3A 6
Briar Way DY13: Stour S 5B 14
Bricast Est. DY13: Stour S 5B 14
Brickyard La. B80: Stud 5C 32
Bridal Rd. B61: D'frd 4A 18
Bridge Rd. B60: B'gve 6D 22
Bridge St. B97: Redd 4F 27
DY10: Kidd 5E 7
DY13: Stour S 4H 13
Bridgnorth Rd. DY11: Kidd 1A 6
Bridley Moor Rd. B97: Redd 4E 27
Brierley Rd. B60: B'gve 3F 23
Brimstone La. B61: D'frd 3A 18
Brindley St. DY13: Stour S 1H 13
Brinklow Cl. B98: Redd 2D 32
Brinton Cl. DY11: Kidd 1C 10
Brinton Cres. DY11: Kidd 1C 10
Britannia Cl. B98: Redd 5H 27
Britannia Gdns. DY13: Stour S 4B 14
British Mills B97: Redd 3G 27
Britten St. B97: Redd .4F 27
Broach Rd. DY13: Stour S 5B 14
Broach Rd. Cvn. Pk. DY13: Stour S 5B 14
Broadfields DY9: Hag .2F 17
Broad Ground Rd. B98: Redd 6D 28
Broad Heath Cl. B97: Redd 3D 26
Broadheath Cl. WR9: Droit S 6D 24
Broadmeadow WR9: Droit S 4C 24

Broad St. B61: B'gve .1B 22
DY10: Kidd 3E 7
Broadwas Cl. B98: Redd 3C 28
BROADWATERS 1G 7
Broadwaters Dr. DY9: Redd 4G 17
DY10: Kidd 2G 7
Brocket Cl. DY13: Stour S 6G 9
Brockhill Dr. B97: Redd 4B 29
Brockhill La. B97: Redd 1A 26
Brockton Pl. DY13: Stour S 5G 13
Bromfield Rd. B97: Redd 6F 27
BROMSGROVE 2C 22
Bromsgrove Bus Station 2C 22
Bromsgrove Cricket, Hockey & Tennis Club . . .6F 23
Bromsgrove Eastern By-Pass B60: B'gve . . .6E 19
Bromsgrove Golf Cen. 2F 23
Bromsgrove Highway B60: B'gve, Fins, Tard, Tutn . .2F 23
B97: Redd 3A 26
Bromsgrove Indoor Bowls Cen. 5C 22
Bromsgrove Rd. B61: D'frd 4A 18
B80: Stud 1E 33
B97: Redd 5C 26
DY9: Clent, Hag 2H 17
WR9: Droit S, Elmb, Rash 3F 25
Bromsgrove Station (Rail) 5E 23
Bromsgrove St. DY10: Kidd 4E 7
Bromsgrove Technology Pk. B60: B'gve 6D 22
Bromwich La. DY9: Pedm 1G 17
Bronte Dr. DY10: Kidd 4H 7
Bronwen Ingham Ct. DY10: Kidd 3E 7
Brook Cl. B60: B'gve .1E 23
DY10: Kidd 6F 7
Brook Cres. DY9: Hag 3G 17
Brookdale DY10: Kidd 2F 7
Brookfield Cl. B97: Redd 6F 31
Brook Flds. Cl. B60: Marlb 1F 19
Brookhampton Cl. B97: Redd 6G 31
BROOK HAVEN MENTAL HEALTH UNIT 6D 18
Brookhouse La. B97: Ham G, Redd 6A 30
Brookhouse Rd. B45: B Grn 3H 19
B60: B'wll 3H 19
Brookland Rd. DY9: Hag 4F 17
Brooklands Dr. DY11: Kidd 1D 6
Brooklands La. B98: Redd 3B 28
Brooklands Pk. B98: Redd 3F 29
Brook Retail Pk. B60: B'gve 5D 22
Brook Rd. B61: B'gve .3B 22
B61: F'fld 1A 18
Brookside Cl. B48: A'chu 1H 21
Brookside Dr. B61: Cats 2C 18
Brookside Way DY10: Blak 6A 16
Brook St. B98: Redd 4A 28
DY11: Kidd 4C 6
Brook Va. DY12: Bew .1E 9
Brookvale Cl. B61: B'gve 6E 19
Brookwood Dr. B45: B Grn 2D 20
Broom Cl. B60: B'gve .2E 23
Broom Cres. DY10: Kidd 4G 7
BROOME 6F 17
Broome Ho. DY9: Brme 6F 17
Broome La. DY9: Brme, Clent 6E 17
DY10: Blak 5D 16
Broomfield Cl. DY11: Kidd 3B 6
Broomfield Grn. DY11: Kidd 3C 6
Broomfield Rd. DY11: Kidd 3B 6
Broom Ri. DY10: Kidd .4G 7
Broomsgrove Highway B97: Redd 5B 26
Broomy Cl. DY13: Stour S 1F 13
Brotherton Av. B97: Redd 6B 26
Browning Cl. DY10: Kidd 4H 7
Bruce Rd. DY10: Kidd .3H 7
Brueton Av. B60: B'gve 4D 22
Brueton Dr. B98: Redd 5A 28
Brunel Cl. DY13: Stour S 1A 14
Buckfast Cl. B61: B'gve 3A 22
Buckleys, The B48: A'chu 4H 21
Buckleys Grn. B48: A'chu 4H 21
Bull Ring DY10: Kidd .4E 7
Bulls Head Yd. B49: Alc 5B 36
Bullus Rd. DY13: Stour S 1A 14
Bumble Hole La. B61: Bourn, D'frd 3B 18
Buntsford Dr. B60: Stoke H 6B 22
Buntsford Ga. Bus. Pk. B60: Stoke H 6B 22
Buntsford Hill B60: Stoke H, Stoke P 6B 22
Buntsford Pk. Rd. B60: B'gve 5H 7
Burcher Grn. DY10: Kidd 5H 7
BURCOT 6E 19
Burcot Av. B60: B'gve 6E 19
Burcot Ho. B60: B'gve 1E 23
(off Burcot La.)
Burcot La. B60: B'gve, Burc 1E 23
(not continuous)
Burghley Dr. DY11: Kidd 5B 6
Burial La. B97: Ham G 6A 30
Burlington Cl. DY10: Kidd 6G 7
Burlish Cl. DY13: Stour S 6G 9
Burlish Crossing DY13: Stour S 6G 9
BURLISH PARK 6G 9
Burlish Top Nature Reserve 4H 9
Burltons Ter. DY12: Bew 1D 8
Burns Cl. B97: Redd 2E 31
DY10: Kidd 4H 7
Burnthorne La. DY13: Dunl, Stour S 6D 12
Burnt Mdw. Rd. B98: Redd 2E 29
Burrington Cl. B97: Redd 3E 27
Burrish St. WR9: Droit S 3E 25
(not continuous)

Burton La. B98: Redd .5H 27
Bushley Cl. B98: Redd 3A 32
Butler's Hill La. B97: Redd 3D 26
Butler St. B96: A'wd B 3A 34
Butler Best Way DY10: Kidd 2D 6
Buttercup Cl. DY11: Kidd 2E 7
Buttercup Dr. B60: Lick E 4F 19
Buttermere Cl. DY13: Stour S 6H 9
Butter St. B49: Alc 6C 36
Butts, The WR9: Droit S 4C 24
Butt Town Cvn. Pk. DY12: Bew 6D 8
Byford Cl. B98: Redd .6G 27
Byland Cl. B61: B'gve .3B 22
Byron Cl. DY10: Kidd .5H 7
Byron Rd. B97: Redd .2F 31
Byron Way B61: Cats .2D 18

C

Cairndhu Dr. DY10: Kidd 3G 7
Calder Cl. WR9: Droit S 5C 24
Calder Rd. DY13: Stour S 5G 9
Caldwall Cres. DY11: Kidd 5D 6
Caldwall Tower 5E 7
Caldy Wlk. DY13: Stour S 6G 9
Callow Cl. DY13: Stour S 5F 13
CALLOW HILL 4C 30
Callow Hill La. B97: Redd 4B 30
Callow Hill Rd. B48: A'chu 3G 21
Callows La. DY10: Kidd 4E 7
Campden Cl. B97: Redd 4F 31
Camp Furlong WR9: Redd 5C 24
Camp Hill WR9: Droit S 5C 24
(off Bower Hill)
Campion Way DY12: Bew 5F 5
Canalside DY13: Stour S 2B 14
Canal Side Sq. DY10: Kidd 4D 6
(off Weavers Wharf)
Canberra Cl. B61: B'gve 1B 22
Canterbury Cl. B80: Stud 6C 32
Canterbury Rd. DY11: Kidd 3H 5
Captain's Hill B49: Alc 3D 36
Captain's Pool Rd. DY10: Kidd 2G 11
Cardinal Cres. B61: B'gve 3A 22
Cardinal Dr. DY10: Kidd 1H 11
Cardington Cl. B98: Redd 5F 29
Cardy Cl. B97: Redd 1D 30
Carlton Cl. B97: Redd .1D 30
DY11: Kidd 2A 6
Carlyle Av. DY10: Kidd 4H 7
Carlyle Rd. B'gve 4E 23
Carnforth Rd. B60: B'gve 3E 23
Carnoustie Cl. B61: B'gve 3A 22
Carol Av. B61: B'gve 1A 22
Carpet Trades Way DY11: Kidd 3D 6
Carroll Wlk. DY10: Kidd 4H 7
Carter Av. DY11: Kidd .6B 6
Carter Ct. DY11: Kidd .6C 6
Carters Cl. B61: B'gve 5A 22
Carter's Gdns. DY11: Kidd 6A 6
Carthorse La. B97: Redd 3D 26
Castleditch La. B98: Redd 3G 31
Castle La. DY12: Bew .1E 9
Castle Locks DY10: Kidd 5E 7
Castle Rd. B49: Alc 3B 36
B80: Stud 6E 33
DY11: Kidd 5D 6
Castle St. B96: A'wd B 2A 34
CATCHEMS END 5F 5
Cathedral Av. DY11: Kidd 4A 6
Catherine Ct. B60: B'gve 4C 22
Catkins Cl. B61: Cats .1E 19
CATSHILL 2C 18
Cavendish Cl. B60: Marlb 1F 19
Cavendish Dr. DY9: Hag 4E 17
DY10: Kidd 3H 7
Caynham Cl. B98: Redd 4D 28
Cedar Cl. DY13: Stour S 4H 13
WR9: Droit S 6E 25
Cedar Ct. B60: B'gve .1D 22
Cedar Cres. DY11: Kidd 4C 6
Cedar Dr. B60: B'gve .3D 22
DY11: Kidd 3C 6
Cedargrove DY9: Hag .2F 17
Cedar Pk. Rd. B97: Redd 4F 27
Cedar Rd. DY13: Stour S 2G 13
Cedar Rd. B97: Redd .4E 27
Cedar Ter. B60: B'gve .3D 22
Cedar Vw. B97: Redd .4E 27
Celeste Rd. B60: B'gve 3D 22
Celvestune Way WR9: Droit S 5C 24
Cemetery La. B97: Redd 5F 27
Centech Pk. B98: Redd 2F 29
Central Rd. B60: B'gve 2D 22
Chaceley Ct. B97: Redd 2F 31
Chadcote Way B61: Cats 1C 18
Chaddesley Cl. B98: Redd 1H 31
Chaddesley Gdns. DY10: Kidd 5G 7
Chaddesley Rd. DY10: Kidd 5G 7
CHADWICK 6E 15
Chadwick Bank Ind. Est. DY13: C'wick 6D 14
Chadwick La. DY11: Hartl 4E 15
DY13: C'wick 6D 14
Chadwick M. B98: Redd 3A 32
Chaffinch Dr. DY10: Kidd 2F 11

Chalverton Ct. WR9: Droit S 5B 24
Champions Way DY3: Kidd 3E 7
Champney DY10: Kidd 2E 11
Chancery M. B60: B'gve 3C 22
Chandlers Cl. B97: Redd 4F 31
Chantry Cres. B49: Alc 5B 36
Chapel Ct. B96: A'wd B 3A 34
  DY10: Kidd 1G 7
Chapel Hill DY10: Kidd 1G 7
Chapel La. B98: Beo 1F 29
  DY13: Stour S 6G 13
Chapel Pl. DY11: Kidd 4D 6
Chapel Rd. B96: A'wd B 3A 34
Chapel St. B60: B'gve 2D 22
  B96: A'wd B 3A 34
  B97: Redd 1F 31
  DY9: Hag 3F 17
  DY11: Kidd 4D 6
Chapel St. Pct. B60: B'gve 2D 22
Chapel Wlk. B60: B'gve 2D 22
Chapman Way B49: Alc 3C 36
CHARFORD 5B 22
Charford Rd. B60: B'gve 4B 22
Charland Ct. WR9: Droit S 1C 24
Charlecote Cl. B98: Redd 6D 28
Charlecot Rd. WR9: Droit S 5F 25
Charles Av. DY10: Kidd 1G 7
Charles Dickens Cl. WR9: Redd 6D 24
Charles Henry Rd. WR9: Droit S 3F 25
Charles Martin Bus. Pk. B98: Redd 4A 28
Charles St. B97: Redd 1E 31
  DY10: Kidd 4F 7
Charlotte Bronte Dr. WR9: Droit S 6D 24
CHARLTON 3E 15
Charlton La. DY11: Hartl, Tort 3E 15
Chatterton Wlk. DY10: Kidd 4H 7
Chaucer Cres. DY10: Kidd 4H 7
Chaucer Rd. B60: B'gve 4E 23
CHAWSON 5C 24
Chawson La. WR9: Droit S, Salw 5B 24
Chawson Pleck WR9: Droit S 4C 24
Chawson Rd. WR9: Droit S 4D 24
CHAWSON VALLEY 5B 24
Cheapside DY13: Stour S 4A 14
Chedworth Cl. B98: Redd 3C 28
Chelmarsh Cl. B98: Redd 1C 28
Cheltenham Av. B61: Cats 1E 19
Chepstow Dr. B61: Cats 1E 19
Chequers Cl. DY13: Stour S 6H 13
Cherington Cl. B98: Redd 1F 33
Cherrington Gdns. DY9: Pedm 1H 17
Cherry Cl. DY12: Bew 1B 8
  WR9: Droit S 5G 25
Cherry Cres. B61: B'gve 2B 22
Cherry Gro. B45: B gro 2D 20
Cherry Hill Av. B45: B Grn 2D 20
Cherry Hill Dr. B45: B Grn 2D 20
Cherry Hill Rd. B45: B Grn 2C 20
Cherry Orchard DY10: Kidd 5F 7
Cherry Orchard Dr. B61: B'gve 1B 22
Cherry Tree Wlk. B97: Redd 4D 26
  DY13: Stour S 6G 13
Cheshire Gro. DY11: Kidd 3A 6
Chesshire Av. DY13: Stour S 6G 13
Chesshire Cl. DY13: Stour S 6G 13
Chester Rd. Nth. DY10: Kidd 2F 7
Chester Rd. Sth. DY10: Kidd 2E 11
Chesterton Cl. B97: Redd 6F 31
Chestnut Ct. B49: Alc 5C 36
  B96: Sam 1D 34
  DY11: Kidd 2B 6
Chestnut Dr. DY9: Hag 3E 17
Chestnut Gro. DY11: Kidd 2B 6
Chestnut Rd. B61: B'gve 6C 18
  B96: A'wd B 3A 34
Chestnut Spinney WR9: Droit S 6E 25
Chestnut Walk DY11: Kidd 1C 10
Cheswick Cl. B98: Redd 5G 29
Chesworth Rd. B60: B'gve 2E 23
Cheviot Cl. DY13: Stour S 6F 13
Chichester Av. DY11: Kidd 1C 6
Chillingworth Ho. B97: Redd 3F 27
Chiltern Cl. DY13: Stour S 6F 13
Chirk Cl. DY10: Kidd 2E 11
Chorley Rd. WR9: Droit S 3E 25
Church Av. DY13: Stour S 2A 14
Church Cl. B96: A'wd B 2A 34
Church Down Cl. B97: Redd 4F 31
Church Dr. DY13: Stour S 2A 14
Churchfield Ct. B97: Redd 6B 26
CHURCHFIELDS .1C 22
Churchfields B61: B'gve 1C 22
  DY10: Kidd 3E 7
Churchfields Bus. Pk. DY10: Kidd 3E 7
Churchfields Gdns. B61: B'gve 1C 22
Churchfields Rd. B61: B'gve 1C 22
Church Grn. E. B97: Redd 4G 27
  B98: Redd 4G 27
Church Grn. W. B97: Redd 4G 27
CHURCH HILL 4B 16
Church Hill B98: Beo 2D 28
Church Hill Way B98: Redd 3B 28
CHURCHILL 4B 16
Churchill & Blakedown Golf Course 6A 16
Churchill Av. WR9: Droit S 5D 24
Churchill Forge 4B 16

Churchill La. DY10: Blak, C'hll 6A 16
Churchill Rd. B61: Cats 1D 18
Church La. B61: B'gve 2C 22
Church Rd. B61: B'gve 1C 22
  B61: Cats 2C 18
  B96: A'wd B 2A 34
  B97: Redd 4F 27
            (Adelaide St.)
  B97: Redd 6A 26
            (Foxlydiate La.)
  WR9: Droit S 2F 25
Churchstone Cl. B61: Cats 2C 18
Church St. B49: Alc 5C 36
  B61: B'gve 2C 22
  B80: Stud 1G 35
  DY9: Hag 3F 17
  DY10: Kidd 4E 7
Church Vw. DY12: Bew 1C 8
Church Wlk. DY11: Kidd 4C 6
  DY13: Stour S .4G 13
Circus, The DY10: Kidd 4D 6
            (off Weavers Wharf)
Cirencester Cl. B60: B'gve 3E 23
Cladsworth Ho. B97: Redd 4C 26
            (off Poplar Rd.)
Claerwen Av. DY13: Stour S 5G 9
Claines Cres. DY10: Kidd 5H 7
Clarence Cl. DY10: Kidd 4F 7
Clarence Way DY12: Bew 6D 4
Clarendon Ct. B97: Redd 3D 26
Clare Cl. B97: Redd 4C 6
Clare Witnell Cl. DY11: Kidd 2B 6
Clarke St. B97: Redd 4F 27
Claughton Cl. DY11: Kidd 5C 6
Claughton St. DY11: Kidd 5C 6
Claverdon Cl. B97: Redd 6F 31
Claybrook Dr. B98: Redd 3E 33
Clayfields La. B97: Ham G 6A 30
Clayhall Rd. WR9: Droit S 5F 25
Claypit La. B61: Bourn 1B 18
Clayton Dr. B60: B'gve 5E 23
Clearwell Rd. B98: Redd 5C 28
Clee Av. DY11: Kidd 2C 10
Cleeve Cl. B98: Redd 3D 28
  DY13: Stour S 6F 13
Clee Vw. WR9: Droit S 4D 24
Clement Dalley Dr. DY11: Kidd 2D 10
Clensmore St. DY10: Kidd 3D 6
Clent Av. B97: Redd 3F 31
  DY11: Kidd 3B 10
Clent Dr. DY9: Hag 2H 17
Clent Ho. B60: B'gve 1E 23
            (off Burcot La.)
Clent M. DY11: Kidd 3B 10
Cleobury Cl. B97: Redd 2D 26
Cleobury Rd. DY12: Bew 2A 8
Clews Rd. B98: Redd 3H 31
Clifford Cl. WR9: Droit S 6A 24
Clifford Rd. WR9: Droit S 6A 24
Clifton Cl. B98: Redd 1D 32
Clifton Rd. DY10: Kidd 3A 10
Clive Rd. B60: B'gve 4E 23
  B97: Redd 4F 27
Clock House, The B61: Bourn 3B 18
Cloisters, The B80: Stud 6D 32
Clydesdale Cl. WR9: Droit S 6G 25
Clydesdale Ri. WR9: Droit S 6G 25
Clydesdale Rd. WR9: Droit S 6G 25
Coach Cotts. B45: B Grn 2E 21
Coates Rd. DY10: Kidd 3H 7
Cobden St. DY11: Kidd 4C 6
Cobham Cl. B60: B'gve 5C 22
Cobham Ct. WR9: Droit S 4E 25
Cobham Ct. M. DY9: Hag 2H 17
Cobham Cres. DY12: Bew 1C 8
Cobham Rd. DY10: Kidd 6E 7
Cobley Hill B48: A'chu 6F 21
Cobnall Rd. B61: Cats 1D 18
Cockshute Hill WR9: Droit S 4G 25
Cockshutt La. B61: D'frd 4A 18
Coconut Island 5B 28
Cofton Cl. B97: Redd 3D 26
Cold Comfort La. B49: Alc 4A 36
Coldfield Dr. B98: Redd 2F 31
Colebrook Cl. B49: Alc 5C 36
Coleford Cl. B97: Redd 6C 26
Colemeadow Rd. B98: Redd 2E 29
Coleridge Cl. B97: Redd 2E 31
Coleshill Cl. B97: Redd 6E 31
Colford Cl. WR9: Droit S 5B 24
College Grn. WR9: Droit S 5D 24
College Rd. B60: B'gve 2D 22
  DY10: Kidd 6E 7
College Wlk. B60: B'gve 2D 22
            (not continuous)
  DY10: Kidd 6E 7
Collier Cl. DY11: Kidd 1C 10
Collins Way B49: Alc 1A 32
Collinson Cl. B98: Redd 4D 36
Collis Cl. B60: B'gve 5B 22
Colman Rd. WR9: Droit S 3E 25
Colts La. B98: Redd 5D 28
COMBERTON 5H 7
Comberton Av. DY10: Kidd 5H 7
Comberton Gdns. DY10: Kidd 6G 7
Comberton Gdns. DY10: Kidd 5H 7

Comberton Hgts. DY10: Kidd 5F 7
            (off Comberton Ter.)
Comberton Hill DY10: Kidd 5F 7
Comberton Mans. DY10: Kidd 5G 7
Comberton Pk. Rd. DY10: Kidd 6H 7
Comberton Pl. DY10: Kidd 5F 7
Comberton Rd. DY10: Kidd 5F 7
Comberton Ter. DY10: Kidd 5F 7
Common La. B80: Map G 5H 29
Commonside DY13: Stour S 6G 13
Compass Way B60: B'gve 5D 22
Compton Cl. B97: Redd 3E 31
Conference Way DY13: Stour S 1G 13
Congleton Cl. B97: Redd 6F 31
Conifer Gro. B61: B'gve 1C 22
Conifer Pl. DY13: Stour S 2B 14
Coningsby Dr. DY11: Kidd 3A 6
Coniston Cl. B60: B'gve 3E 23
Coniston Cres. DY13: Stour S 6H 9
Coniston Ho. DY10: Kidd 3E 7
Coniston Way DY12: Bew 1A 8
Connaught Av. DY11: Kidd 1C 10
Connaught Rd. B60: B'gve 3F 23
Consort Gdns. B61: B'gve 1D 22
Conway Rd. B60: B'gve 3C 22
Cookridge Cl. B97: Redd 3E 27
Cooper Cl. B60: B'gve 6B 22
Coopers Hill B48: A'chu 4E 21
Coopers La. DY13: Stour S 3H 13
Copcut Cl. WR9: Droit S 5C 24
Copcut Golf Cen. 6A 24
Copcut Ct. WR9: Droit S 5C 24
Copcut La. WR9: Cop, Salw . . . . . .5A 24 & 6A 24
Cope Gdns. DY13: Stour S 5F 13
Coppice, The DY8: Hag 3E 17
Coppice Cl. B97: Redd 5E 27
  WR9: Droit S 1C 24
Coppice Hgts. DY11: Kidd 3B 10
Coppice Trad. Est. DY11: Kidd 4B 10
Coppice Way WR9: Droit S 1B 24
Corbett Av. WR9: Droit S 5E 25
Corbett Cl. B60: B'gve 4E 23
Corbett Rd. DY11: Kidd 2A 6
Corbett St. WR9: Droit S 4E 25
Cordle Marsh Rd. DY12: Bew 5E 5
Corinthian Ct. B49: Alc 5C 36
Cormorant Gro. DY10: Kidd 1H 11
Corndon Cl. DY11: Kidd 3B 10
Corner La. B97: Redd 6A 26
Cornerways DY12: Bew 1B 8
Cornfield Av. B60: Stoke H 6A 22
Cornhampton Cl. B97: Redd 3D 26
Cornmill Gdns. B60: B'will 5B 20
Cornwall Av. DY11: Kidd 1C 6
Cornwell Cl. B98: Redd 5B 32
Coronation Ter. B60: B'gve 4E 23
Coronation Way DY10: Kidd 5H 7
Coroner's Court
            Stourport-on-Severn 2A 14
Corporation St. DY10: Kidd 5E 7
Cosford Cl. B98: Redd 1F 33
Costers La. B98: Redd 2G 33
Cotswold Cl. DY13: Stour S 5F 13
Cotswold Cl. DY11: Kidd 2C 10
Cotswold Way B61: B'gve 5D 18
Cottage Dr. B60: Marlb 1G 19
Cottage Farm La. B60: Marlb 1F 19
Cottage La. B60: Marlb 1F 19
Cotton Pool Rd. B61: B'gve 2B 22
COUGHTON 6H 35
Coughton Court .6H 35
Coughton Hill B49: Cou 6H 35
Counting Ho. Way B60: Stoke H 6B 22
County La. DY8: I'ley 1C 16
Court Cl. DY11: Kidd 1B 6
Court Dr. DY13: Stour S 2H 13
Courtney DY10: Kidd 2E 11
Courtyard, The B97: Redd 6C 22
Coventry Highway B98: Redd 4H 27
Coventry St. DY10: Kidd 4E 7
Covercroft WR9: Droit S 3E 25
Covers, The B80: Stud 4E 33
Covert, The DY11: Kidd 3B 6
Cowper Wlk. DY10: Kidd 4H 7
Cowslip Cl. B61: Cats 1C 18
Cox Ho. DY9: Hag 3G 17
CRABBS CROSS .4F 31
Crabbs Cross La. B97: Redd 5F 31
Crabtree Cl. B98: Redd 6H 27
  DY9: Hag 2G 17
Crabtree Ct. B61: B'gve 1B 22
Crabtree Dr. B61: B'gve 1B 22
Crabtree La. B61: B'gve 6B 18
Cradley Cl. B98: Redd 1F 33
Cranberry Dr. DY13: Stour S 2G 13
Crane St. DY11: Kidd 4C 6
Cranham St. B97: Redd 2D 30
Creed Cl. DY9: Hag 3H 17
Crendon Cl. B80: Stud 5E 33
Crescent, The B60: B'gve 3C 22
  DY8: Hag 3E 17
  DY11: Kidd 4F 11
Crescent Ho. B97: Redd 4C 6
            (off Mt. Pleasant)
Crescent Rd. DY11: Kidd 4C 6
Crestwood Av. DY11: Kidd 5A 6

Croft, The B60: Stoke H 6B 22
DY10: Blak 6B 16
DY11: Kidd 6A 6
Croft Cl. B98: Redd 5D 28
Crofters Cl. WR9: Droit S 1C 24
Crofters Grn. WR9: Droit S 1C 24
(off Crofters Way)
Crofters Hill WR9: Droit S 1C 24
Crofters Way WR9: Droit S 1C 24
Crooks La. B49: Alc 3C 36
B80: Stud 6D 32
Crooks La. Bus. Pk. B80: Stud 6D 32
Croome Cl. B98: Redd 1F 33
Cropthorne Cl. B98: Redd 3A 32
Cropthorne Ho. B60: B'gve 1E 23
(off Burcot La.)
Crosbie Gro. DY11: Kidd 2C 10
Crossgate Rd. B98: Redd 2C 32
Cross Keys M. DY9: Hag 4E 17
Crossley Retail Pk. DY11: Kidd 3D 6
Crossley Wlk. B60: B'gve 5B 22
Cross Rd. B49: Alc 5B 36
Cross Cl. B61: B'gve 2C 22
Crownhill Mdw. B61: Cats 5F 25
Crown La. DY8: I'ley 1B 16
DY10: Kidd 6E 15
DY11: Ware 6G 15
DY13: C'wick, C'way G 6E 15
Crown Mdw. B48: A'chu 4H 21
Crowther St. DY11: Kidd 4C 6
CRUISE HILL 6A 30
Cruise Hill La. B97: Elc B, Ham G 5A 30
Crumpfields La. B97: Redd 2A 30
Crundalls La. DY12: Bew 3D 4
Crutch La. WR9: Droit S 2F 25
WR9: Elmb 1F 25
Cullum Cl. B80: Stud 1F 35
Curlew Cl. DY10: Kidd 1C 8
Curr La. B97: Bks G, Redd 5A 26
Cutty Sark Dr. DY13: Stour S 4B 14
Cygnet Cl. B48: A'chu 3H 21
Cygnet Ct. DY10: Kidd 3G 11
Cypress Ct. DY10: Kidd 6G 7
Cypress Ho. B60: B'gve 2D 22
Cyprus Av. B96: A'wd B 2A 34

D

Dagnell End Rd. B98: Redd 1G 27
DAGTAIL END 1A 34
Dagtail La. B97: Redd 6F 31
Dairy La. B97: Redd 3C 26
Dale Cl. B61: Bourn 3C 18
Dale Hill B60: B'wll 4A 20
Dale La. B60: B'wll, Lick E 3H 19
Dale Rd. B98: Redd 3H 27
Damson Cl. B97: Redd 4E 31
Damson Way DY12: Bew 6E 5
Danescroft DY13: Stour S 3A 14
Danube Cl. WR9: Droit S 6C 24
Danzey Cl. B98: Redd 5B 32
Dark La. B60: Stoke H 6A 22
B96: A'wd B 3A 34
Davenham Rd. B60: B'gve 3F 23
Davenport Dr. B60: B'gve 3E 23
David Lloyd Leisure
Bromsgrove 1E 23
David's Cl. B97: Redd 6F 27
Dawson Rd. B61: B'gve 2A 22
Daybrook Cl. B97: Redd 3D 26
Deans Cl. B98: Redd 3D 28
Deanscroft Dr. B60: Lick E 4F 19
Deansway B61: B'gve 3A 22
Deansway, The DY10: Kidd 3G 7
Deansway Ho. DY10: Kidd 2G 7
Deer Barn Hill B98: Redd 1A 32
Deerhurst Cl. B98: Redd 1C 28
Defford Cl. B97: Redd 1A 30
Delamere Rd. DY12: Bew 6E 5
Dell, The DY13: Stour S 2C 14
Dellow Gro. B48: A'chu 5H 21
Delphinium Cl. DY11: Kidd 1C 6
Denehurst Cl. B45: B Grn 1B 20
Derrick Burcher's Mall DY10: Kidd 4E 7
Derwent Av. DY13: Stour S 1H 13
Derwent Dr. DY12: Bew 6B 4
Derwent Gro. WR9: Droit S 5B 24
Derwent Ho. DY10: Kidd 3F 7
Derwent Way B60: B'gve 5D 22
Design Cl. B60: B'gve 2H 9
Devil's Spittleful & Rifle Range Nature Reserve
....1C 6
Devon Cl. DY11: Kidd 1C 6
Devonish Cl. B49: Alc 3C 36
Devonport Cl. B97: Redd 3D 26
Dewberry Cl. DY13: Stour S 2G 13
Dewsbury Cl. B96: A'wd B 3A 34
Didcot Cl. B97: Redd 5E 31
Dilwyn Cl. B98: Redd 1F 33
Dinedor Cl. B98: Redd 5D 28
Dingleside B98: Redd 6G 27
Dinmore Cl. B98: Redd 5D 28
Discovery Rd. DY13: Stour S 4B 14
Ditchford Cl. B97: Redd 6F 31
Dixon Cl. B97: Redd 3F 27
Dixon Ct. DY10: Hurc 2H 7

Dixon St. DY10: Kidd 5E 7
Dock, The B61: Cats 2D 18
Doctors Hill B61: Bourn 1A 18
Dodderhill Rd. WR9: Droit S 2F 25
Dodford Ho. B60: B'gve 1E 23
(off Burcot La.)
Dodford Rd. B61: Bourn 1A 18
Duebank Dr. DY6: A'wd B 1A 34
Dog La. DY12: Bew 1D 8
Dolben La. B98: Redd 5D 28
Dolphin Centre, The 2D 22
Dolphin Rd. B98: Redd 3A 28
Domar Rd. DY11: Kidd 3B 6
Donnington Cl. B98: Redd 3B 28
Dordale Rd. B61: Bourn 1A 18
Dormston Cl. B98: Redd 1H 31
Dorothy Terry Ho. B97: Redd 2F 31
Dorridge Cl. B97: Redd 1D 30
Dorsett Rd. DY13: Stour S 1H 13
Dotterel Pl. DY10: Kidd 3G 11
Dove Cl. DY10: Kidd 2H 11
Dovecote Cl. B97: Redd 2E 27
Dovecote Rd. B61: B'gve 3B 22
WR9: Droit S 5F 25
Doverdale Av. DY10: Kidd 5H 7
Doverdale Cl. B98: Redd 3B 32
WR9: Droit S 4D 24
Dowlers Hill Cres. B98: Redd 2A 32
DOWLES 5B 4
Dowles DY12: Bew 5A 4
DOWLES BROOK 5A 4
Dowles Cft. WR9: Droit S 3D 24
Dowles Rd. DY11: Kidd 2B 10
DY12: Bew 3A 4
Downsell Ho. B97: Redd 6B 26
Downsell Rd. B97: Redd 6C 26
Dragoon Flds. B60: B'gve 4E 23
Drake Cres. DY11: Kidd 3H 5
Drakes Cl. B97: Redd 4E 31
Draycott Cl. B97: Redd 2D 32
Drayton Cl. B98: Redd 6D 28
Drayton Cl. B60: B'gve 4E 23
Driffield Cl. B98: Redd 6D 28
Drive, The B98: Redd 5G 27
Droitwich Community Woods 4B 24
Droitwich Golf Course 1G 25
Droitwich Rd. DY10: Harti, Shens, Tort 5G 11
DY11: Tort 5G 11
DROITWICH SPA 3E 25
DROITWICH SPA BMI HOSPITAL 3E 25
Droitwich Spa Heritage Cen. 3E 25
(off Victoria Sq.)
Droitwich Spa Leisure Cen. 3C 24
Droitwich Spa Station (Rail) 3D 24
Drovers Grn. WR9: Droit S 1C 24
(off Shepherds Hill)
Drovers Pl. WR9: Droit S 1C 24
Drovers Wlk. DY10: Kidd 5F 7
Drovers Way DY10: Kidd 6R 22
WR9: Droit S 1C 24
Drummond Rd. B60: B'gve 4E 23
Dry Mill La. DY12: Bew 5A 4
Dudley St. DY10: Kidd 3E 7
Dugard Way WR9: Droit S 6A 24
Dugdale Cl. DY9: Hag 3G 17
Dulais Cl. B98: Redd 1G 31
Dunbar Cl. DY12: Bew 4H 7
Dunchurch Cl. B98: Redd 1F 33
Dunclent Cres. DY10: Kidd 5H 7
Dunedin Dr. B45: B Grn 1B 20
Dunhampton Dr. DY10: Kidd 1H 7
DUNLEY 6D 12
Dunley Gdns. DY13: Stour S 4G 13
Dunley Rd. DY12: Heigh 4A 12
DY13: Dunl 4A 12
DY13: Dunl, Stour S 6D 12
Dunlin Dr. DY10: Kidd 2F 11
Dunlop Rd. B97: Redd 5E 31
Dunmore Rd. DY12: Bew 5E 5
Dunnington Av. DY10: Kidd 1G 7
Dunstall Cl. B97: Redd 6C 26
Durham Cl. B61: B'gve 6B 18
Durrant M. DY9: Hag 4G 17
Dursley La. B98: Redd 5G 29
Dusthouse La. B60: Fins, Tard 6F 23
Duxford Cl. B97: Redd 2D 30
DW Fitness
Kidderminster 4E 7
Dwyer Cl. DY9: Hag 3G 17
Dyas Cl. DY9: Hag 3G 17

E

Eadie M. B97: Redd 1F 31
Eagle Rd. B98: Redd 3E 29
Eardisley Cl. B98: Redd 1F 33
Earls Cl. B97: Redd 6B 26
Early River Pl. DY12: Bew 1B 8
Easemore Rd. B98: Redd 4G 27
Easenhall La. B98: Redd 1E 33
EASTERN HILL 2B 34
Eastern Hill B96: A'wd B 2A 34
Easter Pk. DY11: Kidd 3F 11
Eastham Cl. DY12: Bew 1D 8
(off Severn Side Sth.)
Eastham Pl. B98: Redd 2A 32

Easthope Cl. DY13: Stour S 6G 13
E. Moons Ho. B98: Redd 4E 29
E. Moons Moat Ind. Area B98: Redd 3E 29
Eastnor Cl. B98: Redd 1G 31
DY10: Kidd 3E 11
East Pk. Dr. WR9: Droit S 2C 24
East Rd. B60: B'gve 3D 22
DY13: Stour S 1A 14
East St. DY10: Kidd 4F 7
Eastwood Cl. B96: A'wd B 3A 34
Eastwood Dr. DY10: Kidd 6H 7
Eathorpe Cl. Redd 2E 33
Echells Cl. B61: B'gve 2A 22
Eckington Cl. B98: Redd 2B 32
Eclipse Rd. B49: Alc 4A 36
Eden Cl. B80: Stud 1F 35
Edenfield Cl. B97: Redd 1A 30
Edgewood Dr. B45: B Grn 1C 20
(not continuous)
Edgeworth Cl. B98: Redd 3C 28
Edgioake La. B96: A'wd B 6A 34
EDGIOCK 6A 34
Edgmond Cl. B98: Redd 4D 28
Edinburgh Cl. DY10: Kidd 2E 7
Edrell La. B60: B'gve 3C 22
Edward St. B97: Redd 4F 27
Edwin Av. DY11: Kidd 3E 11
Edwin Ct. B60: B'gve 4C 22
Edwin Cres. B60: B'gve 4C 22
Egret Ct. DY10: Kidd 3G 11
Eider Cl. DY10: Kidd 3H 11
Elan Av. DY13: Stour S 5G 9
Elan Cl. DY12: Bew 1B 8
ELCOCK'S BROOK 5A 30
Elderberry Cl. DY13: Stour S 2G 13
Eldersfield Cl. B98: Redd 1E 29
Eldorado Cl. B80: Stud 6D 32
Elgar Cl. B97: Redd 2E 31
Elgar Cres. WR9: Droit S 6E 25
Elgar M. B60: B'gve 2C 22
Eliot Wlk. DY10: Kidd 4H 7
Elizabeth Av. WR9: Droit S 3F 25
Elizabeth Cl. WR9: Droit S 3F 25
Elizabeth Way B97: Redd 3F 25
Eliza Gdns. B61: Cats 1E 19
Ellenbrook Cl. B97: Redd 3D 26
Ellerdene Cl. B98: Redd 2F 31
Ellesmere Dr. DY12: Bew 1B 8
Elm Ct. B97: Redd 4F 27
Elmdale Dr. DY10: Kidd 5H 7
Elm Dr. B49: Ove G 5D 36
DY10: Blak 6A 16
Elmfield Rd. DY11: Hartl 5G 15
Elmfield Wlk. DY13: Stour S 2F 13
Elm Gro. B61: B'gve 6D 18
DY13: Stour S 6F 13
Elmhurst Cl. B97: Redd 6F 31
Elmley Cl. DY11: Kidd 1B 10
Elmley Ho. B97: Redd 4C 26
(off Lock Cl.)
Elm Rd. B97: Redd 4C 27
B98: Redd 4G 7
Elms Cl. B60: B'gve 5E 23
Elmstone Cl. B97: Redd 2E 27
Elrington Cl. B97: Redd 2E 27
Elton Rd. DY12: Bew 1B 8
Elvington Cl. B98: Redd 1F 33
Ely Cl. DY11: Kidd 4A 6
Emery Ct. DY10: Kidd 3E 7
Emperor Pl. DY10: Kidd 5G 7
(off Oxbow Way)
Empire Ct. B97: Redd 3G 27
Endeavour Pl. DY13: Stour S 4A 14
ENFIELD 3F 27
Enfield Cl. B60: B'gve 5B 22
Enfield Cl. B98: Redd 4G 31
Enfield Ind. Est. B97: Redd 3F 27
Enfield Rd. B97: Redd 5F 31
(not continuous)
Engadine Rd. B60: B'gve 3F 23
Engine Cl. B60: B'gve 5E 23
Engine La. DY13: Stour S 3H 13
Enid Blyton Cnr. WR9: Droit S 6D 24
Ennerdale Rd. DY13: Stour S 6H 9
Ennerdale Rd. DY13: Stour S 2E 31
Epsom Cl. B97: Redd 2E 31
Epsom Rd. B61: Cats 1D 18
Erica Cl. DY11: Kidd 1D 6
Erneley Cl. DY13: Stour S 5H 13
Erwood Cl. B97: Redd 6D 26
Eton Wlk. DY9: Hag 2F 17
Ettingley Cl. B98: Redd 5B 32
Eunal Ct. B97: Redd 5G 31
(off Well Cl.)
Evenlode Cl. B98: Redd 1H 31
Evergreen Way DY13: Stour S 2B 14
Evertons Cl. WR9: Droit S 5D 24
Evesham Ho. B60: B'gve 1E 23
(off Burcot La.)
Evesham M. B97: Redd 5G 27
(off Kingfisher Shop. Cen.)
Evesham Rd. B96: A'wd B 1A 34
B97: Redd 1F 31
Evesham Sq. B97: Redd 5G 27
(off Kingfisher Shop. Cen.)
Evesham St. B49: Alc, Arr 6A 36
B97: Redd 5G 27

Evesham Wlk. B97: Redd 4G 27
Ewloe Cl. DY10: Kidd 3E 11
Exchange St. DY10: Kidd 5E 7
Exeter Cl. DY11: Kidd 4A 6
Exhall Cl. B98: Redd 3D 28
Exmoor Cl. B61: B'gve 6D 18
Exmoor Dr. B61: B'gve 6D 18
Eyton Cl. B98: Redd 5D 28

F

Fabricius Av. WR9: Droit S 4E 25
Factory La. B61: B'gve 3B 22
Fairbourne Gdns. B97: Redd 2E 31
Fairfield Ho. B60: B'gve 1E 23
                              (off Burcot La.)
Fairfield Rd. B61: Bourn 1A 18
Fairford Cl. B98: Redd 1E 29
Fairlight Dr. B45: B Grn 1B 20
Fairmont Rd. B60: B'gve 4E 23
Fairoak Dr. B60: B'gve 6B 22
Fairview Cotts. B48: A'chu 4G 21
                             (off Birches La.)
Fairwater Cres. B49: Alc 4D 36
Fairways Ct. DY10: Kidd 6G 7
Fairways Dr. B60: B'wll 5B 20
Fairweather Cl. B97: Redd 2E 27
Falcon Cl. DY10: Kidd 1E 11
       WR9: Droit S 6G 25
Falconry Centre, The 5E 17
Falling Sands DY11: Kidd 2D 10
Fallowfields Cl. B61: B'gve 1B 22
FALSAN PITTS
Falstaff Dr. WR9: Droit S 6D 24
Fantastico 5E 7
Farfield DY10: Kidd 5F 7
Farlow Cl. B98: Redd 5D 28
Farm Cl. DY11: Kidd 2B 10
Farmcote Cl. B97: Redd 6F 31
Farmers Ct. WR9: Droit S 1C 24
Farmers Grn. WR9: Droit S 1C 24
Farmers Piece WR9: Droit S 1C 24
                            (off Farmers Ct.)
Farmers Rd. B60: B'gve 6B 22
Farmers Way WR9: Droit S 1C 24
Far Moor La. B98: Redd 3F 29
Farm Rd. B98: Redd 5A 28
       DY13: Stour S 1B 14
Farnborough Cl. B98: Redd 1F 33
Farrier Cl. B60: B'gve 6B 22
Farriers Cl. WR9: Droit S 2C 24
Farriers Cnr. WR9: Droit S 2C 24
Farriers Sq. WR9: Droit S 2C 24
                            (off Farriers Cl.)
Farriers Way WR9: Droit S 2C 24
Farthing La. B97: Redd 3D 26
Fearnings Cotts. B97: Redd 5F 31
Featherbed La. B97: Redd 5D 30
Feathers Ct. DY13: Stour S 2A 14
Feckenham Ho. B60: B'gve 1E 23
                             (off Burcot La.)
Feckenham Rd. B96: A'wd B 2A 34
       B97: Redd 6D 30
                               (Blaze La.)
       B97: Redd 2E 31
                             (Tennyson Rd.)
Feel Good Health Club 5F 5
Felix Baxter Dr. DY11: Kidd 2C 10
Felton Cl. B98: Redd 1E 33
Fen Cl. DY10: Kidd 2E 7
Fenwick Cl. B49: Alc 3D 36
       B97: Redd 1D 30
Ferguson Dr. DY11: Kidd 3A 10
Ferndale Cl. B61: Cats 1D 18
       DY9: Hag 3F 17
       DY13: Stour S 3C 14
Ferndale Cres. DY11: Kidd 2A 6
Ferndale Ga. B60: B'wll 5B 20
Ferndale Housing Est. DY11: Kidd 2A 6
Ferney Hill Av. B97: Redd 5E 27
Fernleigh B60: B'gve 3D 22
                             (off New Rd.)
Fernwood Cl. B98: Redd 5B 32
Field Cl. B60: Stoke H 6B 22
Field End DY13: Stour S 2G 13
Fieldfare Ct. DY10: Kidd 3G 11
Field Farm La. B98: Redd 6D 28
Field La. DY9: Clent 4H 17
Fields Pk. Dr. B49: Alc 4D 36
Fiery Hill Rd. B45: B Grn 3D 20
Fiery Hill Rd. B45: B Grn 2C 20
Findon Cl. B97: Redd 3C 26
Findon St. DY10: Kidd 4F 7
Finepoint DY11: Kidd 4B 10
Finepoint Way DY11: Kidd 4B 10
FINSTALL 3G 23
Finstall Rd. B60: B'gve, Fins 4E 23
Fircroft Cl. B60: Stoke H 6A 22
Firecrest Way DY10: Kidd 3H 11
Firenze Rd. B60: B'gve 4F 23
Firs, The B98: Redd 6G 27
       WR9: Droit S 4C 24
Firs Cl. B60: Marlb 1F 19
Firs Cl., The DY10: Kidd 5G 7
Firs Ind. Est. DY11: Kidd 5B 10
Fir Tree Cl. B97: Redd 4F 27

Fisher Rd. B49: Kinw 3D 36
Fish Hill B97: Redd 4G 27
Fishing Line Rd. B97: Redd 3G 27
Fit4Less
       Redditch 4C 28
Fladbury Cl. B98: Redd 2B 32
Flanders Cl. B98: Redd 3D 28
Flats, The B61: B'gve 1C 22
Flavel Rd. B60: B'gve 5B 22
Flax Cl. B49: Alc 5B 36
Flaxley Cl. B98: Redd 4G 29
Fleetwood Cl. B97: Redd 6C 26
Flint Cl. DY10: Kidd 2E 11
Florence Av. WR9: Droit S 5D 24
Flyford Cl. B98: Redd 1H 31
Fockbury Mill La. B61: B'gve, D'frd 5A 18
Fockbury Rd. B61: D'frd 4A 18
Foley Av. DY11: Kidd 4C 10
Foley Bus. Pk. DY11: Kidd 4C 10
Foley Dr. DY11: Kidd 4C 10
Foley Gro. DY11: Kidd 4B 10
Foley St. DY11: Kidd 1C 10
FOLEY PARK 1C 10
Folly, The B97: Redd 2F 31
Fordbridge Cl. B97: Redd 1E 31
FORDBROOK 1F 15
Fordhouse Rd. B60: B'gve 3D 22
Ford La. WR9: Elmb 1G 25
Ford Rd. B61: B'gve 3B 22
Foredraught B80: Stud 6E 33
Foredrift Cl. B98: Redd 1G 31
Foregate St. B96: A'wd B 3A 34
Forelands Gro. B61: B'gve 4A 22
Forest Cl. B60: Lick E 4E 19
       DY12: Bew 1B 8
Forester Way DY10: Kidd 1E 11
Forest Vw. B97: Redd 4F 31
Forge Av. B60: B'gve 5E 23
Forge Cl. B61: Cats 1D 18
Forge Ct. DY13: Stour S 2A 14
                           (off St Michael's Cl.)
Forge La. B61: Blak 1C 22
Forge La. DY10: Kidd 6A 16
Forge Mill Needle Mus. 2H 27
Forge Mill Rd. B98: Redd 3H 27
Fort Mahon Pl. DY12: Bew 1B 8
Forward Cotts. B48: A'chu 4G 21
                            (off Withybed La.)
Foster Av. B80: Stud 1F 35
Foundry St. DY13: Stour S 2A 14
Four Acres Cvn. Pk. DY13: Stour S 4B 14
Four Oaks Cl. B98: Redd 2F 31
Four Oaks Dr. B61: Marlb 1E 19
Fowler Pl. DY13: Stour S 1A 14
Fownhope Cl. B98: Redd 5E 29
Foxcote Cl. B98: Redd 4E 29
Foxes Cl. B60: B'wll 5C 20
Foxglove Way B60: Lick E 4F 19
Foxhill Barns B48: A'chu 4F 21
Foxhill La. B48: A'chu 4E 21
Foxholes, The DY10: Kidd 2F 7
Foxhollow B61: B'gve 4A 22
Foxhunter Cl. WR9: Droit S 6G 25
Fox La. B61: B'gve 5A 26
FOXLYDIATE 5A 26
Foxlydiate Cl. B97: Redd 5C 26
Foxlydiate Cres. B97: Redd 4B 26
Foxlydiate La. B97: Redd 6A 26
Foxlydiate M. B97: Redd 4C 26
                             (off Lock Cl.)
Foxtail Pl. B61: Cats 2E 19
Foxwalks Av. B61: B'gve 4A 22
FRANCHE 2B 6
Franche Ct. DY11: Kidd 1B 6
Franche Ct. Dr. DY11: Kidd 1B 6
Franche Rd. DY11: Kidd 2B 6
Franchise St. DY11: Kidd 5C 6
Francis Rd. B60: B'gve 5C 22
       DY13: Stour S 6G 9
Frank Freeman Ct. DY10: Kidd 2F 7
Frankton Cl. B98: Redd 2E 33
Freda Eddy Ct. DY10: Kidd 4E 7
Frederick Early Ho. B98: Redd 3B 32
Frederick Rd. DY11: Kidd 3E 11
Freeman Ct. DY11: Kidd 1B 10
Friar St. WR9: Droit S 3E 25
Friday Acre WR9: Droit S 5C 24
Fringe Grn. B60: B'gve 5D 22
Fringe Grn. Cl. B60: B'gve 5D 22
Fringe Mdw. Rd. B98: Redd 2F 29
Frith Cl. DY9: Hag 3G 17
Front Cotts. B48: A'chu 4G 21
Fulbrook Cl. B98: Redd 3C 28
Fulmar Cres. DY10: Kidd 2H 11
Fulton Cl. B60: B'gve 3E 23
Furlong, The WR9: Droit S 1E 25
Furrows, The B60: Stoke H 6A 22
Furze, The B98: Redd 4G 29

G

Gainsborough M. DY11: Kidd 5B 6
Gala Dr. DY13: Stour S 1G 13
Galahad Way DY13: Stour S 2H 13
Galton Way WR9: Had 4H 25

Gamson Cl. DY10: Kidd 6E 7
Ganborough Rd. B97: Redd 1E 33
Garden Cl. B60: B'gve 6D 22
Gardeners Cl. DY11: Kidd 2C 6
Gardners Mdw. DY12: Bew 1D 8
Garganey Ct. DY10: Kidd 3F 11
Garibaldi Ter. B60: B'gve 3D 22
Garland Rd. DY13: Stour S 6F 9
Garrick Rd. B60: B'gve 3F 23
Garrington Rd. B60: B'gve 5E 23
Garway Cl. B98: Redd 1E 33
Gas Ho. La. B49: Alc 5C 36
Gas Sq. B61: B'gve 3B 22
Gateacre Dr. B45: B Grn 4A 34
Gatehouse Cvn. Pk. DY13: Stour S 5B 14
Gate Ho. La. B60: B'gve 5D 22
Gateley Cl. B98: Redd 4G 29
Gaudet Luce Golf Course 6H 25
Gauge Cl. DY11: Kidd 5D 22
Gaunts, The B48: A'chu 1H 21
Gaydon Cl. B98: Redd 1H 31
Gemini Bus Pk. DY10: Kidd 3C 10
Geoffrey Chaucer Wlk. WR9: Droit S ..6D 24
George Baylis Rd. WR9: Droit S 2D 24
George Rd. B48: A'chu 4H 21
       B60: B'gve 6D 22
George St. B61: B'gve 2C 22
       DY10: Kidd 4F 7
George Wlk. B97: Redd 5G 27
                          (off Kingfisher Shop. Cen.)
Georgian Cl. B49: Alc 4B 36
Georgian Way DY10: Kidd 3D 6
Gerard Rd. B49: Alc 3D 36
Gheluvelt Av. DY10: Kidd 3F 7
Gheluvelt Ct. DY13: Stour S 2H 13
Gibb La. B61: Cats 2D 18
Gibbons Cres. DY13: Stour S 2H 13
Gibbs Rd. B98: Redd 3A 28
Gilbert Cl. B60: B'gve 5B 22
Gilbert Rd. B60: B'gve 5B 22
Gilbert Scott Way DY10: Kidd 3F 7
Gilbertstone Cl. B98: Redd 1G 31
Gilgal DY13: Stour S 2A 14
Gisburn Cl. B97: Redd 3D 26
Glastonbury Cl. DY11: Kidd 4A 6
Glebe, The B98: Beo 1F 29
Glebe Cl. B98: Redd 6D 28
Glebe Rd. B48: A'chu 3H 21
       B49: Kinw 3D 36
Glen, The B60: B'wll 4B 20
Glendale WR9: Droit S 5C 24
Glendale Ter. B97: Redd 5G 31
Gleneagles Dr. B60: B'wll 5B 20
Glenfield Cl. B97: Redd 4F 31
Globe Ct. B49: Alc 5B 36
Gloucester Cl. B97: Redd 4F 27
Gloucester Way DY12: Bew 6D 4
Glover St. B98: Redd 5G 27
Godson Cres. DY11: Kidd 1B 10
Godson Pl. DY11: Kidd 1C 10
Goldcrest Dr. DY10: Kidd 2H 11
Golden Cross La. B61: Cats 1D 18
Golden Hind Dr. DY13: Stour S 4A 14
Goldsmith Wlk. DY10: Kidd 5H 7
Goldthorn Cl. DY11: Kidd 2C 10
Goldthorne Ct. B97: Redd 1E 31
Goldthorn Pl. DY11: Kidd 2C 10
Goldthorn Rd. DY11: Kidd 1B 10
Goodrich Cl. B98: Redd 6F 29
Goodwin Cl. DY11: Kidd 3C 6
Goodwood Rd. B61: Cats 1E 19
Gooseshill Cl. B98: Redd 1E 33
Gorcott Hill B98: Beo 4H 29
Gordon Anstis Ho. B98: Redd 2D 28
Gordon Pl. DY10: Kidd 5F 7
Gorse Cl. WR9: Droit S 6F 25
Gorsemeadow Dr. B45: B Grn 2C 20
Gorsey Cl. B96: A'wd B 4A 34
Goscote Cl. B97: Redd 2C 26
Gould Av. E. DY11: Kidd 2A 10
Gould Av. W. DY11: Kidd 3A 10
Grafson Pl. WR9: Droit S 5C 24
Grafton Cl. B98: Redd 3B 32
Grafton Cres. B60: B'gve 5B 22
Grafton Ho. B60: B'gve 1E 23
                             (off Burcot La.)
Grafton La. B61: U War 5A 22
Granary Rd. B60: Stoke H 6B 22
Granby Cl. B98: Redd 4F 29
Grange, The B98: Redd 4H 27
                          (off Beoley Rd. W.)
Grange Ct. B98: Redd 4H 27
Grange La. B48: A'chu 6F 21
Grange Rd. B98: Redd 4H 27
       DY11: Kidd 3A 6
                           (Beaufort St.)
       DY11: Kidd 3B 6
                             (Domar Rd.)
Grangers La. B98: Redd 5H 31
Granhill Cl. B98: Redd 2A 32
Granville Cl. B60: B'gve 3E 23
Granville Crest DY10: Kidd 4H 7
Grasmere Gro. DY13: Stour S 6H 9
Gray Cl. DY10: Kidd 4H 7
Grayshott Cl. B61: B'gve 1B 22
Grazing La. B97: Redd 6A 26
Gt. Barn La. B97: Redd 1D 30

Greatfield Rd. DY11: Kidd 6B 6
Gt. Hockings La. B97: Redd 6A 26
Gt. Western Way DY13: Stour S 1A 14
Greatwich Way DY10: Kidd 3D 6
Greaves Gdns. DY11: Kidd 1B 6
Green, The B96: Sam 4E 35
DY9: Hag 1C 17
Greenacres La. DY12: Bew 6C 4
Greenacres Rd. B61: B'gve 1B 22
Greenbank B45: B Grn 2H 35
WR9: Droit S 4G 25
Greenbank Rd. DY12: Bew 1A 8
Green Bower Dr. B61: B'gve 5D 18
Green Cl. B80: Stud .1G 35
Greendale Cl. B61: Cats 2E 19
Greenfield Av. B60: Marlb 1G 19
Greenfields B98: Redd 6G 27
Greenfinch Cl. DY10: Kidd 1H 11
Greenford Cl. B97: Redd 3D 26
GREEN HILL 5A 20
GREENHILL 3G 7
Greenhill B60: B'wll, Burc 6H 19
Greenhill Av. DY10: Kidd 2F 7
Green Hill Cl. B60: Lick E 4G 19
Greenhill Ind. Est. DY10: Kidd 3G 7
Greenhill Oak DY10: Kidd 6E 7
Greenhurst Dr. B45: B Grn 1C 20
GREENLANDS 2H 31
Greenlands Av. B98: Redd 2A 32
Greenlands Bus. Cen. B98: Redd 1B 32
Greenlands Dr. B98: Redd 6H 27
GREEN LANE 4C 32
Green La. B61: Cats 1D 18
B80: Stud 5B 32
B97: Redd 1B 30
WR9: Had 5H 25
Green Lanes Cvn. Pk. DY13: Stour S 4B 14
Green Mdw. DY9: Pedm 1G 17
Green Pk. Rd. B60: B'gve 3E 23
Green Slade Cres. B60: Marlb 1F 19
Green St. DY10: Kidd 6E 7
Green Sward La. B98: Redd 1D 32
Greenway, The DY9: Hag 3E 17
Greig, The 4C 36
Grendon Cl. B98: Redd 1D 32
Greville Rd. B49: Alc 3A 36
Greyfriars Dr. B61: B'gve 2A 22
Grey Grn. La. DY12: Bew 5D 4
Greys Rd. B80: Stud 1G 35
Greystone Cl. B98: Redd 2C 28
Griffin Av. DY10: Kidd 6E 7
Grimley Cl. B98: Redd 1H 31
Grimley La. B60: Fins 5H 23
Grinnall Bus. Cen., The DY13: Stour S 5B 14
Grosvenor Av. DY10: Kidd 4F 7
Grosvenor Cl. WR9: Droit S 5G 25
Grosvenor Cres. WR9: Droit S 5F 25
Grosvenor Gdns. B61: Lick E 5E 19
DY13: Stour S 2A 14
Grosvenor Way WR9: Droit S 5F 25
Grosvenor Wood DY12: Bew 1B 8
Grove, The B80: Stud 1F 35
(not continuous)
DY8: Hag 3E 17
DY13: Stour S 5B 14
Grove Gdns. B61: B'gve 4D 18
Grove St. B98: Redd 4G 27
Guardian Ct. B60: B'gve 2D 22
Guild Ct. B60: B'gve 2C 22
Guildford Cl. DY11: Kidd 4A 6
Guild Rd. B60: B'gve 3C 22
Guinness Cl. B98: Redd 2F 31
Guiting Cl. B97: Redd 1D 30
Gunners La. B80: Stud 6E 33
Gunnings Rd. B49: Alc 4C 36
Gurneys La. WR9: Droit S 3F 25
Guys Wlk. B61: B'gve 5D 18

H

HABBERLEY 4A 6
Habberley Golf Course 1G 5
Habberley La. DY11: Kidd, Low H 2H 5
Habberley Rd. DY11: Kidd 3A 6
DY12: Bew 5F 5
Habberley St. DY11: Kidd 4C 6
Habberley Valley DY11: Kidd, Low H 2G 5
Habershon Ct. WR9: Had 4H 25
Hadlow Cl. B98: Redd 5A 36
Hadrians Wlk. B49: Alc 5H 25
HADZOR 4C 26
Hadzor Ho. B97: Redd 4C 26
Hadzor La. WR9: Had 4G 25
Hafren Cl. DY12: Bew 1D 8
Hafren Way DY13: Stour S 2H 13
HAGLEY 2H 17
Hagley Cl. DY9: Hag 2H 17
Hagley Grange DY9: Hag 2G 17
Hagley Ho. B60: B'gve 1E 23
(off Burcot La.)
Hagley Station (Rail) 3F 17
HALES PARK 2B 8
Hales Pk. DY12: Bew 1B 8
Halifax Ct. DY11: Kidd 2A 6
Hall Dr. DY9: Hag 2H 17
HALL FLAT 3F 19

Hall La. DY9: Hag 2H 17
Halls Farm La. DY12: Trim 2D 4
HAM GREEN 6A 30
Ham Grn. La. B97: Elc B, Ham G 5A 30
Hamilton Cl. B60: Lick E 4F 19
Hamilton Dr. B80: Stud 1F 35
Hamilton Rd. B97: Redd 2E 31
DY11: Kidd 1B 10
Hammond Cl. WR9: Droit S 5F 25
Hammond Ct. WR9: Had 4H 25
Hampton Av. B60: B'gve 4D 22
Hampton Cl. B98: Redd 3B 32
Hampton Rd. WR9: Droit S 2E 25
Hanbury Cl. B60: B'gve 4D 22
Hanbury Ho. B97: Redd 4D 26
(off Cardy Cl.)
Hanbury Rd. B60: Stoke H, S Prior 6A 22
WR9: Droit S 3F 25
Hanbury St. WR9: Droit S 3F 25
Hanover Cl. DY12: Bew 1C 8
Hanover Ct. B97: Redd 2F 31
Hanover Pl. B61: B'gve 3C 22
Hanover St. B61: B'gve 2C 22
Hanstone Rd. DY13: Stour S 5H 13
Harberrow Cl. DY9: Hag 2F 17
Harbours Cl. B61: B'gve 5A 22
Harbury Cl. B98: Redd 1D 32
Hardwick La. B80: Stud 5G 33
Hardy Av. DY10: Kidd 4G 7
Haresfield Cl. B97: Redd 6F 27
Hargreaves Ct. DY11: Kidd 1B 10
Harland Cl. B61: B'gve 1A 22
Harlech Way DY10: Kidd 2E 11
Harold Davies Dr. DY13: Stour S 4H 13
Harold Evers Way DY10: Kidd 3F 7
Harport Rd. B98: Redd 1A 32
Harpswell Av. B98: Redd 2B 32
Harriers Grn. DY10: Kidd 2H 7
Harris Cl. B98: Redd 3D 24
WR9: Droit S 3F 25
Harris Hill WR9: Droit S 3E 25
Harrison Rd. B97: Redd 2E 31
Harrow Cl. B60: Stoke H 6B 22
DY9: Hag 2F 17
Harry Taylor Ho. B98: Redd 5A 28
Hartford Rd. B61: B'gve 4E 23
HARTLEBURY 4H 15
Hartlebury Castle 3F 15
Hartlebury Cl. B98: Redd 1D 28
Hartlebury Common (Nature Reserve) 4C 14
Hartlebury Rd. DY13: Stour S 3B 14
Hartlebury Station (Rail) 4H 15
Hartlebury Trad. Est. DY10: Hartl 4H 15
Harvest Cl. B60: Stoke H 6A 22
Harvington Cl. B97: Redd 3D 26
DY11: Kidd 2A 6
Harvington Rd. B60: B'gve 4D 22
Haseley Cl. B98: Redd 1E 33
Haselor Cl. B49: Alc 4D 36
Hastings Ct. DY13: Stour S 2A 14
Hastings Rd. B60: B'gve 5B 22
Hatfield Cl. B98: Redd 1E 33
Hatton Cl. B98: Redd 2B 32
Haven, The B45: B Grn 2B 20
Hawfinch Ri. DY10: Kidd 2G 11
Hawford Av. DY10: Kidd 5G 7
Hawford Pl. WR9: Droit S 5C 24
HAWKBATCH 1A 4
Hawksbury Cl. B98: Redd 3D 28
Hawkstone Cl. DY11: Kidd 2D 6
Hawksworth Ho. DY10: Kidd 5F 7
Hawthorn Cl. B49: Alc 3B 36
Hawthorn Coppice DY9: Hag 2F 17
Hawthorne Wlk. WR9: Droit S 6E 25
Hawthorn Gro. DY11: Kidd 4A 6
Hawthorn Rd. B61: B'gve 5D 18
B97: Redd 4C 26
Hawthorns, The DY9: Hag 4E 17
(off Cavendish Dr.)
DY10: Kidd 5G 7
Haybridge Av. DY8: Hag 3E 17
Haybridge M. DY9: Hag 2E 17
Haybridge Sports Cen. 3C 6
Hay Cl. DY11: Kidd 4C 6
Haydock Rd. B61: Cats 1E 19
Haydon Cl. B80: Stud 6E 33
Haydon Way B49: Cov 3H 35
Haye La. B80: Map G 1G 33
Hayford Cl. B98: Redd 3A 28
Hayloft Cl. B60: Stoke H 6B 22
Haynes Cl. B61: Cats 2E 19
Haynes Ho. B97: Redd 6F 27
(off Mt. Pleasant)
Hazel Cl. WR9: Droit S 6E 25
Hazeldene DY13: Stour S 3C 14
Hazel Rd. B97: Redd 3E 27
Hazels, The DY9: Hag 4E 17
(off The Greenway)
Hazelton Cl. B61: Marlb 2F 19
Hazelton Rd. B61: Marlb 2E 19
Hazlewood Cl. DY11: Kidd 6A 6
Hazlewood Cl. B49: Alc 5A 36
HDA Sports & Social Club 4D 26
HEADLESS CROSS .2F 31
Headless Cross Dr. B97: Redd 1F 31
Headley Ct. B97: Redd 2F 31

HEATH, THE 5G 5
Heath Cl. B60: Stoke H 6B 22
Heath Dr. DY10: Kidd 1H 7
Heathfield Cres. DY11: Kidd 6B 6
Heathfield Rd. B97: Redd 1B 30
DY12: Bew 6E 5
DY13: Stour S 5B 14
Heathlands, The DY12: Stour S 4B 14
Heath La. DY10: Stone 3H 11
Hedera Rd. B98: Redd 2F 29
Hedgerow Cl. B98: Redd 2H 31
Hedges Way B60: B'gve 3E 23
Heightington La. DY13: Dunl 6C 12
Heightington Rd. DY12: Heigh, Ribb 3A 12
Heming Rd. B98: Redd 3E 33
Hemmings Entry B97: Redd 4G 27
Hemming St. DY11: Kidd 6C 6
Henley Ct. B49: Alc .4C 36
Henley Dr. WR9: Droit S 5F 25
Henley Rd. B80: Map G 6H 29
Henley St. B49: Alc .4C 36
Hennals Av. B97: Redd 6B 26
Henry Wlk. B60: B'gve 5B 22
Hentland Ct. B98: Redd 4D 28
Herbert Austin Dr. B60: Marlb 1H 19
Herbert St. B98: Redd 4G 27
Hereford Cl. B49: Alc .5A 6
Heriotts Ct. WR9: Droit S 3F 25
Heriotts La. WR9: Droit S 3F 25
(not continuous)
Heritage Way WR9: Droit S 3E 25
Hermitage Way DY13: Stour S 5G 13
Herne's Nest DY12: Bew 2C 8
Heron Cl. B48: A'chu 3H 21
B49: Alc 3B 36
Heronfield Cl. B98: Redd 2C 28
Heronswood Rd. DY10: Kidd 2F 11
Herons, The WR9: Droit S 3F 25
Hertford Rd. B49: Alc .5A 6
Hewell Av. B60: B'gve 5C 22
Hewell La. B45: B Grn 2D 20
B60: Tard 3A 26
HEWELL PARK 2A 26
Hewell Pl. B45: B Grn 2E 21
(off Hewell Rd.)
Hewell Rd. B45: B Grn 2E 21
B97: Redd 3E 27
Heydon Rd. B60: Fins 3G 23
Highclere DY12: Bew .2C 8
Highclere Dr. DY12: Bew 2C 8
Highfield Av. B97: Redd 2E 31
Highfield Cl. WR9: Droit S 4E 25
Highfield Rd. B61: B'gve 4B 22
B80: Stud 6D 32
B97: Redd 2F 31
DY10: Kidd 2G 7
Highfields B61: B'gve 3B 22
Highgate Cl. DY11: Kidd 6A 6
Highgrove Cl. DY10: Kidd 1G 7
HIGH HABBERLEY 3H 5
Highlands Cl. DY11: Kidd 5A 6
Highland Way B98: Redd 2A 32
Highley Cl. B98: Redd 2B 10
DY11: Kidd 2B 10
Highlow Av. DY11: Kidd 1C 6
High Mdws. B60: Stoke H 6A 22
HIGH PARK 4A 24
High St. B49: Alc 5B 36
B61: B'gve 6E 33
B80: Stud 6E 33
B96: A'wd B 3A 34
DY10: Kidd 4E 7
DY12: Bew 1D 8
DY13: Stour S 3A 14
WR9: Droit S 3E 25
High Trees Cl. B98: Redd 3G 31
Hilda Peers Way DY12: Bew 1C 8
Hillary Rd. DY13: Stour S 5D 10
Hillcarinie Ho. WR9: Droit S 4E 25
(off St Andrew's Rd.)
Hill Cl. DY11: Kidd 5A 6
HILL CREST GRN 4C 32
Hillcroft Cvn. Pk. DY12: Bew 1A 8
Hillditch La. DY11: Hartl 4E 15
HILL END 2F 25
Hillend WR9: Droit S 2F 25
(off Bromsgrove Rd.)
Hillgrove Ct. DY11: Kidd 4D 6
Hill Gro. Cres. DY11: Kidd 5G 7
Hillgrove Gdns. DY10: Kidd 6G 7
Hill La. B60: B'gve 3C 22
Hillmeadow Vw. B96: A'wd B 3A 34
Hillmorton Cl. B98: Redd 2E 29
Hill Rise Vw. B60: Lick E 4G 19
Hills, The B98: Redd 1C 28
Hillside B98: Redd 2E 29
Hillside Cl. DY13: Stour S 6G 13
Hillside Dr. B61: Lick E 4E 19
DY11: Kidd 3A 6
Hill St. DY11: Kidd 4D 6
HILL TOP 3A 22
Hill Top B97: Redd .1B 30
Hilltop Av. DY12: Bew .6F 5
Hillview Cl. B60: Lick E 4F 19
Hillview Rd. B60: Lick E 4F 19

Himbleton Cl. B98: Redd 1H 31
Hindlip Cl. B98: Redd 4G 29
Hinton Av. B48: A'chu 4H 21
Hinton Flds. B61: Bourn 3B 18
Hipkiss Gdns. WR9: Droit S 2D 24
Hither Grn. La. B98: Redd 1H 27
HMP Hewell B97: Redd 1A 26
Hoarstone DY8: Hag 3E 17
Hoarstone Cl. DY12: Bew 5E 5
Hoarstone La. DY12: Bew, Trim 3E 5
Hodfar Rd. DY13: Stour S 5B 14
Hollies, The B45: B Grn 1B 20
DY13: Stour S 6G 9
Hollington Ho. B97: Redd 3F 27
Hollington Rd. B48: A'chu 1H 21
Holloway, The WR9: Droit S 3F 25
Holloway Cl. WR9: Droit S 4F 25
Holloway Cl. DY10: Kidd 5F 7
(off George St.)
Holloway Dr. B98: Redd 6H 27
Holloway La. B98: Redd 5H 27
Holloway Pk. B98: Redd 5A 28
Hollowfields Cl. B98: Redd 1G 31
Hollyberry Cl. B98: Redd 4G 29
Holly Cl. WR9: Droit S 6F 25
Holly Ct. DY10: Kidd 2D 6
(off Alder Av.)
Hollyfield Dr. B45: B Grn 1B 20
Holly Gro. B61: B'gve 6C 18
Holly Rd. B61: B'gve 6C 18
DY13: Stour S 2B 14
Holman St. DY11: Kidd 5C 6
Holmcroft Rd. DY10: Kidd 4G 7
Holmwood Av. DY11: Kidd 4A 6
Holmwood Dr. B97: Redd 5E 27
Holmwood Ho. B97: Redd 5E 27
HOLT END 1F 29
Holt Gdns. B80: Stud 2G 35
Holt Hill B98: Beo 1F 29
Holt Rd. B80: Stud 2G 35
Holyoakes Cl. B98: Redd 2E 29
Home Mdw. La. B98: Redd 6E 29
Home Piece WR9: Droit S 4C 24
Homestead WR9: Droit S 5C 24
Homfray Rd. DY10: Kidd 1F 7
Honeybrook Gdns. DY11: Kidd 1B 6
Honeybrook Cl. DY11: Kidd 1B 6
Honeybrook Ter. DY11: Kidd 1B 6
Honeychurch Cl. B98: Redd 5H 27
Honeymans Gdns. WR9: Droit S 2D 24
Honeysuckle Cotts. B48: A'chu 4G 21
HOOBROOK 2F 11
Hoobrook Ent. Cen. DY10: Kidd 2E 11
Hoobrook Ind. Est. DY10: Kidd 2E 11
Hoo Farm Ind. Est. DY11: Kidd 3F 11
Hoopers La. B96: A'wd B 3A 34
Hoo Rd. DY10: Kidd 6E 7
Hopgardens Av. B60: B'gve 2E 23
Hopkins Precinct, The B49: Alc 4C 36
Hop Pole La. DY12: Bew 1A 8
Hopton Dr. DY10: Kidd 3E 11
Hopyard La. B98: Redd 5D 28
Hornbeam Cl. DY12: Bew 1A 8
Hornbeam Ho. DY12: Bew 1A 8
HORNGROVE 4G 11
Horse Fair DY10: Kidd 3E 7
Horton Cl. B49: Alc 3C 36
Housman Cl. B60: B'gve 4B 22
Housman Cl. B60: B'gve 2D 22
(off Housman Pk.)
Housman Pk. B60: B'gve 2D 22
Housman Wlk. DY10: Kidd 4H 7
Hoveton Cl. B98: Redd 1B 32
Howard Av. B61: B'gve 1B 22
Howard Rd. B98: Redd 2B 32
Huband Cl. B98: Redd 3A 28
Huins Cl. B98: Redd 4A 28
Hume St. DY11: Kidd 5C 6
Humphrey Av. B60: B'gve 5B 22
Humphries Dr. DY10: Kidd 2F 11
HUNT END 5E 31
Hunt End Ind. Est. B97: Redd 5E 31
Hunt End La. B97: Redd 5E 31
Hunters Cl. WR9: Droit S 2C 24
Hunters Cl. B98: Redd 6A 28
(off Shakespeare Av.)
Hunters End WR9: Droit S 2C 24
Hunters Grn. WR9: Droit S 2C 24
Hunters Pl. WR9: Droit S 2C 24
Hunters Way WR9: Droit S 2C 24
Huntington Cl. B98: Redd 6E 29
Hunts Ri. DY12: Bew 1E 9
HURCOTT 2H 7
Hurcott Cl. DY10: Kidd 3F 7
Hurcott La. DY10: Hurc 1H 7
Hurcott Rd. DY10: Hurc, Kidd 3E 7
Hurcott Village DY10: Hurc 2H 7
Husum Way DY10: Kidd 3H 7
Hyde Cl. B60: B'gve 2E 23

I

Ibis Cl. DY10: Kidd 1H 11
Ibstock Cl. B98: Redd 4E 29
Ibstock Ho. B98: Redd 4E 29
Icknield Row B49: Alc 4A 36

Icknield St. B98: Beo 1C 28
B98: Redd 6D 28
Icknield St. Dr. B80: Redd 6D 28
B98: Redd 6D 28
Ideal Bldgs. DY11: Kidd 4D 6
Illshaw Cl. B98: Redd 4G 29
Ilmington Cl. B98: Redd 1D 32
Imber Rd. DY10: Kidd 3G 11
Imex Bus. Cen. B98: Redd 4E 29
Imperial Av. DY10: Kidd 2F 7
Imperial Ct. DY10: Kidd 2F 7
Imperial Gdns. DY10: Kidd 2F 7
Imperial Gro. DY10: Kidd 2F 7
Impney Cl. B98: Redd 2D 28
Impney Grn. WR9: Droit S 3G 25
Impney Way WR9: Droit S 3G 25
Inett Way WR9: Droit S 3B 24
Ingeva Dr. B45: B Grn 1B 20
Ingram Cres. DY12: Bew 6C 4
Inn La. DY11: Hartl 4G 15
Insetton Cl. B98: Redd 4D 28
IPSLEY 6D 28
Ipsley Chu. La. B98: Redd 6C 28
Ipsley La. B98: Redd 6D 28
Ipsley Mnr. B98: Redd 6C 28
Ipsley St. B98: Redd 5G 27
Ironside Cl. DY12: Bew 1B 8
Iron Way B60: B'gve 5E 23
Isaacs Way WR9: Droit S 6B 24
Isidore Rd. B60: B'gve 6D 22
Island Dr. DY10: Kidd 6E 7
Ismere Way DY10: Kidd 1G 7
IVERLEY 1C 16
Iverley La. DY8: I'ley 4B 16
Ivor Rd. B97: Redd 6F 27
Ivor White Dr. DY10: Kidd 3E 7

J

Jackdaw La. WR9: Droit S 6G 25
Jackfield Cl. B98: Redd 1E 33
Jackson Cres. DY13: Stour S 5G 13
Jacob's Ladder DY11: Low H 1F 5
Jade Dr. DY9: Hag 3G 17
Jakemans Cl. B98: Redd 4E 29
James Rd. DY10: Kidd 2G 7
Jasmine Gro. B61: B'gve 6C 18
Jay Pk. Cres. DY10: Kidd 2G 11
Jays Cl. B98: Redd 5G 29
Jelleyman Cl. DY11: Kidd 4B 6
Jennings Wood La. DY12: Heigh 3B 12
DY13: Dunl 3B 12
Jephcott Cl. B49: Alc 4A 36
Jersey Cl. B97: Redd 1D 28
Jerusalem Ct. DY10: Kidd 3E 7
Jill La. B80: Stud 3B 34
B96: Sam 3B 34
Jinnah Rd. B98: Redd 6G 27
Jinx Cl. DY9: Hag 3G 17
John's Cl. B80: Stud 6C 32
Johnson Cl. B98: Redd 3A 28
Jordan Cl. DY11: Kidd 4B 6
Jordans Cl. B97: Redd 4F 31
Jorden's Wlk. DY12: Bew 6F 5
Joseph Perkins Cl. B96: A'wd B 2A 34
Josiah Mason Mall DY10: Kidd 4E 7
Jotham Cl. DY11: Kidd 2C 10
Jubilee Av. B97: Redd 3F 31
Jubilee Cl. B49: Alc 3C 36
Jubilee Dr. Nth. DY11: Kidd 2B 10
Jubilee Dr. Sth. DY11: Kidd 2B 10
Julian Cl. B61: Cats 2D 18
Junction Rd. B61: B'gve 1B 22
Juniper Ct. DY10: Kidd 6G 7

K

Kateshill DY12: Bew 2D 8
Kateshill Ho. DY12: Bew 2D 8
Kathleen Fld. Ct. B61: B'gve 1C 22
Katmandu Rd. B60: B'gve 3F 23
Katrine Rd. DY13: Stour S 5G 9
Keats Ho. B97: Redd 2E 31
Keats Pl. DY11: Kidd 4H 7
Keele Dr. B98: Redd 2D 28
Keith Winter Cl. B61: B'gve 4C 18
Kelvin Cl. DY11: Kidd 2A 6
Kemble St. B98: Redd 2B 32
Kemerton Ho. B97: Redd 4C 26
KEMP HOSPICE 4C 6
Kempsey Cl. B98: Redd 3B 32
Kempsford Cl. B98: Redd 4H 31
Kempton Cl. B61: Cats 1D 18
Kenchester Cl. B98: Redd 6E 29
Kendal Cl. B60: B'gve 3E 23
B98: Redd 5G 29
Kendal Dr. B45: Coft H 1E 21
Kendal End Rd. B45: B Grn, Coft H ..1E 21
Kendlewood Rd. DY10: Kidd 1H 7
Kenilworth Cl. B97: Redd 2H 7
Kenilworth Dr. DY10: Kidd 2E 11
Kennedy Cl. DY10: Kidd 4H 7
Kenneth Vincent Cl. B97: Redd 6G 31
Ken Somner Gdns. B98: Redd 5A 28
Kent Cl. DY10: Kidd 1E 11

Kentmere Rd. B60: B'gve 3E 23
Kenyon Cl. B60: B'gve 3D 22
Kerry Cft. Cl. B97: Redd 5G 31
Kerry Hill B60: Stoke H 6B 22
Kerswell Cl. B97: Redd 3D 26
Kestrel Cl. DY10: Kidd 1E 11
Kestrel Vw. B60: Lick E 2F 19
KIDDERMINSTER 4E 7
Kidderminster Bus Station 5E 7
Kidderminster Golf Course 6F 7
Kidderminster Harriers FC 6F 7
KIDDERMINSTER HOSPITAL AND TREATMENT CENTRE
....5C 6
Kidderminster Railway Mus. 5F 7
Kidderminster Rd. B61: B'gve, D'frd .1A 22
DY7: I'ley 2A 16
DY9: Hag 3F 17
DY10: I'ley 2A 16
DY12: Bew 1D 8
WR9: Droit S, H Lov 1C 24
Kidderminster Rd. Sth. DY9: Hag 5D 16
Kidderminster Station (Rail) 5F 7
Kidderminster Town Station
Severn Valley Railway 5F 7
Kidderminster Trade Pk. DY10: Kidd .3G 7
Kiln Cl. B80: Stud 6C 32
Kiln Cl. B48: A'chu 5H 21
Kilpeck Cl. B98: Redd 6F 29
Kimberley Cl. B98: Redd 1B 28
Kimbolton Dr. B60: B'wll 5B 20
Kineton Cl. B98: Redd 1D 32
King Charles Cl. DY11: Kidd 4C 6
King Charles Sq. DY10: Kidd 4E 7
King Edward Av. B61: B'gve 6C 18
King Edward Rd. B61: B'gve 5C 18
Kingfisher Bus. Pk. B98: Redd 5A 28
Kingfisher Ct. B48: A'chu 3H 21
WR9: Droit S 3F 25
(off Woodfield Rd.)
Kingfisher Gro. DY10: Kidd 1H 11
Kingfisher Shop. Cen. B97: Redd 4G 27
Kingfisher Sq. B97: Redd 4F 27
(off Kingfisher Shop. Cen.)
Kingfisher Wlk. B97: Redd 4F 27
(off Kingfisher Shop. Cen.)
Kingfisher Way B49: Alc 3B 36
King George Av. B61: B'gve 6C 18
WR9: Droit S 5E 25
King George Ct. B61: B'gve 6B 18
Kingham Cl. B98: Redd 4F 29
Kingley Av. B49: Alc 3C 36
Kings Arms La. DY13: Stour S 6G 13
Kingscote Cl. B98: Redd 1D 28
KINGS COUGHTON 2A 36
Kings Coughton La. B49: King C 2A 36
Kingsley Av. B98: Redd 5A 28
Kingsley Sports Cen. 4C 32
King's Rd. DY11: Kidd 4C 6
Kingston Cl. WR9: Droit S 6F 25
Kingstone Pl. B98: Redd 2B 32
Kingsway DY13: Stour S 5G 9
Kinlet Cl. B98: Redd 5E 29
Kinnersley Cl. B98: Redd 5E 29
Kinnersley Rd. B49: Kinw 3D 36
Kinver Av. DY11: Kidd 4A 10
Kinver Dr. DY9: Hag 1H 17
Kinwarton Cl. B49: Kinw 3D 36
Kinwarton Farm Rd. B49: Kinw 2C 36
Kinwarton Rd. B49: Alc 4C 36
Kinwarton Workshops B49: Kinw ...2C 36
Kipling Wlk. DY10: Kidd 4H 7
Kitebrook Cl. B98: Redd 4E 29
Kite La. B97: Redd 3C 26
Kittiwake Dr. DY10: Kidd 1H 11
Klark Ind. Pk. DY11: Kidd 4B 10
Knightsford Cl. B97: Redd 6B 26
Knottesford Cl. B80: Stud 1E 35
Knowesley Cl. B60: B'gve 2E 23
Knowle Cl. B98: Redd 2C 28
Kylemilne Way DY13: Stour S 3C 14

L

Laburnum Cl. B98: Redd 6G 27
Laburnum Gro. B61: B'gve 6C 18
DY11: Kidd 2B 6
Ladbrook Cl. B98: Redd 3G 31
Ladygrove Cl. B98: Redd 2A 32
Lady Harriet's La. B98: Redd 4H 27
Lahn Dr. WR9: Droit S 6C 24
LAKES, THE 1B 8
Lake's Cl. DY11: Kidd 3C 6
Lakes Cl. DY12: Bew 1B 8
LAKESIDE 5A 28
Lakeside B97: Redd 1A 26
Lakeside Ind. Est. B98: Redd 5A 28
Lakeside Trad. Cen. B98: Redd 4A 28
Lakes Rd., The DY12: Bew 1B 8
Lambourne Dr. DY12: Bew 6B 4
Lancaster Rd. DY12: Bew 1B 8
Lancelot Ho. DY11: Hurc 2H 7
Land Oak Dr. DY10: Kidd 3G 7
Land Oak Dr. DY10: Kidd 2H 7
Landor Rd. B98: Redd 1A 32
Lands End Way DY12: Bew 6C 4
Lane End Wlk. DY13: Stour S 6H 13

Laneside Gdns. DY12: Bew ...1B 8
Langdale Rd. DY13: Stour S ...5F 13
Langford Ct. DY12: Bew ...5E 5
Langley Cl. B98: Redd ...1D 32
Langley Rd. WR9: Droit S ...5F 25
Langsdowne Cres. B80: Stud ...1F 35
Lansdowne Rd. B80: Stud ...1F 35
Lapwing Cl. DY10: Kidd ...5B 6
Lapworth Cl. B98: Redd ...3H 31
Larch Cl. B49: Alc ...3B 36
Larches, The WR9: Droit S ...4E 25
Larches Cott. Gdns. DY11: Kidd ...1C 10
Larches Rd. DY11: Kidd ...1D 10
Larchmere Dr. B61: B'gve ...1B 22
Larch Way DY13: Stour S ...3A 14
Larford Wlk. DY13: Stour S ...5H 13
Larkfield Rd. B98: Redd ...1A 32
LARKHILL ...2E 7
Larkhill DY10: Kidd ...3E 7
Larkhill Ind. Est. DY10: Kidd ...2E 7
Larkin Gdns. DY10: Kidd ...4H 7
Lassington Cl. B98: Redd ...4E 29
Latchford Cl. B98: Redd ...2E 29
Latimer Rd. B48: A'chu ...5H 21
Laurel Bank M. B60: B'wll ...6D 24
Laurel Cl. B98: Redd ...6G 27
Laurel Gdns. B45: B Grn ...6G 27
Laurel Gro. B61: B'gve ...6C 18
Laurelwood Cl. WR9: Droit S ...6G 25
Laurelwood Rd. WR9: Droit S ...6F 25
Lawley Way WR9: Droit S ...6D 24
Lawnswood Ho. DY13: Stour S ...2A 14
Lawrence Gro. DY11: Kidd ...2C 10
Lax Lane DY12: Bew ...1D 8
Laxton Dr. DY12: Bew ...1B 8
Layamon Wlk. DY13: Stour S ...4H 13
Lea, The DY11: Kidd ...5A 6
Lea Bank Av. DY11: Kidd ...5A 6
Lea Castle Cl. DY10: Kidd ...1F 7
Lea Causeway, The DY11: Kidd ...6A 6
Lea Cl. B49: Alc ...3C 36
Lea Cft. Rd. B97: Redd ...5F 31
Leadbetter Dr. B61: B'gve ...2A 22
Lea Pk. Ri. B61: B'gve ...5C 18
Leapgate Av. DY13: Stour S ...1D 14
Leapgate La. DY11: Tort ...1D 14
 DY13: Stour S ...1D 14
Lea St. DY10: Kidd ...5F 7
Leawood Gro. DY11: Kidd ...5A 6
Lechlade Cl. B98: Redd ...1B 28
 (not continuous)
Leckhampton Cl. B97: Redd ...4G 31
Ledbury Cl. B98: Redd ...6F 29
Ledbury Ho. B97: Redd ...4D 26
Ledwych Cl. WR9: Droit S ...3C 24
Ledwych Gdns. WR9: Droit S ...3D 24
Ledwych Rd. WR9: Droit S ...3D 24
Leigh Gro. WR9: Droit S ...2D 24
Lench Cl. B97: Redd ...3C 26
Lenchville DY11: Kidd ...1G 7
Leonard Av. DY10: Kidd ...1G 7
Leswell Gro. DY10: Kidd ...4F 7
Leswell La. DY10: Kidd ...4F 7
Leswell St. DY10: Kidd ...4F 7
Lewkner Almshouses, The B48: A'chu ...5H 21
Leycroft WR9: Droit S ...5E 25
Leysters Cl. B98: Redd ...5E 29
Lichfield Av. DY11: Kidd ...4H 5
Lichfield St. DY13: Stour S ...3A 14
LICKEY END ...4F 19
Lickey Grange B60: Marlb ...1H 19
Lickey Grange Dr. B60: Marlb ...1H 19
Lickey Gro. DY11: Kidd ...2B 10
LICKEY ROCK ...1G 19
Lickey Rock B60: Marlb ...1G 19
LICKEY SQUARE ...1A 20
LICKHILL ...6F 9
Lickhill DY13: Stour S ...2F 13
Lickhill Ind. Est. DY13: Stour S ...2F 13
Lickhill Rd. DY13: Stour S ...2H 13
Lickhill Rd. Nth. DY13: Stour S ...6F 9
Lido, The
 Droitwich Spa ...3F 25
Light La. DY12: Ribb ...3C 8
Lightoak Cl. B97: Redd ...4E 31
Lilac Cl. B98: Redd ...6G 27
 WR9: Droit S ...6F 25
Lilac Gro. DY13: Stour S ...2G 13
Lilleshall Cl. B98: Redd ...5E 29
Lily Grn. La. B97: Redd ...3C 26
Lime Ct. DY10: Kidd ...6G 7
Lime Gro. B61: B'gve ...6C 18
Limekiln Ct. DY10: Kidd ...3D 6
Limes, The B96: A'wd B ...3A 34
Lime Tree Cres. B97: Redd ...4D 26
Lime Tree Wlk. DY13: Stour S ...1G 13
Lincoln Cres. DY11: Kidd ...
Lincoln Rd. B61: B'gve ...6B 18
Lincomb La. DY13: Titt ...6C 14
Linden Av. DY10: Kidd ...3G 7
 DY13: Stour S ...5G 13
Linden Gdns. DY10: Kidd ...4G 7
Linden Gro. DY10: Kidd ...3G 7
Lindridge Cl. B98: Redd ...5G 29
Lineholt Cl. B98: Redd ...4A 32

Linehouse La. B60: Lick E, Marlb ...1G 19
Lingen Cl. B98: Redd ...5E 29
Lingfield Rd. DY12: Bew ...5F 5
Lingfield Wlk. B61: Cats ...1E 19
Links, The DY10: Kidd ...6G 7
Linnet Ri. DY10: Kidd ...3F 11
LINTHURST ...5B 20
Linthurst Newtown B60: B'wll ...5D 20
Linthurst Rd. B45: B Grn ...4B 20
 B60: B'wll ...4B 20
Linton Cl. B98: Redd ...6F 29
Linton M. B98: Redd ...6F 29
Lion Hill DY13: Stour S ...3A 14
Lion Sq. DY10: Kidd ...4E 7
Lion St. DY10: Kidd ...4E 7
Lion Tuery B49: Alc ...5B 36
Lisle Av. DY11: Kidd ...1C 10
Lister Rd. DY11: Kidd ...1B 10
Little Acre B97: Redd ...4F 31
Lit. Forge Rd. B98: Redd ...2C 32
Lit. Grebe Rd. DY10: Kidd ...1H 11
LITTLE HEATH ...4G 19
Littleheath La. B60: Lick E ...4F 19
Little Hill WR9: Droit S ...4B 24
Lit. Hill Ct. WR9: Droit S ...4C 24
Lit. Hill Grn. WR9: Droit S ...4C 24
 (off Little Hill)
Little La. B61: B'gve ...2C 22
Little Orchard WR9: Droit S ...4D 24
 (off Wych Rd.)
Little Park WR9: Droit S ...4C 24
 (off Padgewell Rd.)
LITTLEWOOD GREEN ...2F 35
Littlewood Grn. B80: Stud ...2F 35
Littlewoods B97: Redd ...5F 31
LivingWell Health Club
 Upper Catshill ...1E 19
Llangorse Cl. DY13: Stour S ...5G 9
Llewellyn Cl. DY13: Stour S ...6C 14
Lloyd Ct. B98: Redd ...5G 27
Load St. DY12: Bew ...1D 8
Lobelia Cl. DY11: Kidd ...1C 6
Lock Cl. B97: Redd ...4C 26
Lock Keepers Reach B48: A'chu ...4G 21
Lodge Cl. DY12: Bew ...6F 5
Lodge Cotts. DY13: Stour S ...3A 14
Lodge Cres. DY9: Hag ...6F 5
Lodge Gdns. DY12: Bew ...6H 27
LODGE PARK ...1H 31
Lodge Pool Dr. B98: Redd ...1H 31
Lodge Rd. B98: Redd ...5G 27
 DY13: Stour S ...3A 14
Logan Pl. DY11: Kidd ...2D 10
Lombard St. DY13: Stour S ...3A 14
Long Acre DY10: Kidd ...3F 7
Longboat La. DY13: Stour S ...2A 14
Longborough Cl. B97: Redd ...4D 30
Long Cl. DY9: Hag ...4E 17
Long Compton Dr. DY9: Hag ...2F 17
Longdon Cl. B98: Redd ...3B 32
LONG EYE ...5G 19
Longfellow Cl. B97: Redd ...3E 31
Longfellow Grn. DY10: Kidd ...4H 7
Longhope Cl. B98: Redd ...4G 29
Longland Ct. B61: B'gve ...5B 18
 (off Oldfield Rd.)
Longlands, The B45: B Grn ...3E 21
Long Meadow Rd. B60: Lick E ...4F 19
Longmoor Cl. B98: Redd ...2D 26
Longmynd Way DY13: Stour S ...5F 13
Long Sling WR9: Droit S ...5C 24
Lord Austin Dr. B60: Marlb ...1H 19
Lords La. B80: Stud ...1G 35
Lordswood Cl. B97: Redd ...6B 26
Lorne Gro. DY10: Kidd ...4G 7
Lorne St. DY10: Kidd ...5G 7
 DY13: Stour S ...1A 14
Lovage Rd. B98: Redd ...2F 29
Love Lyne B97: Redd ...4B 30
Lowans Hill Vw. B97: Redd ...4E 27
Lowe La. DY11: Kidd ...1B 6
LOWER CLENT ...4H 17
Lwr. Common La. B97: Redd ...6D 26
Lwr. Gambolds La. B60: Fins ...6E 23
Lwr. Grinsty La. B97: Redd ...3C 30
LOWER HEATH ...5B 14
Lwr. Heath Cvn. Pk. DY13: Stour S ...5B 14
Lwr. Lickhill Rd. DY13: Stour S ...1F 13
LOWER MARLBROOK ...4D 24
Lwr. Meadow WR9: Droit S ...4D 24
 (off Wych Rd.)
Lwr. Mill St. DY11: Kidd ...4D 6
Lower Pk. DY12: Bew ...1D 8
Lower Parklands DY11: Kidd ...5C 6
Lwr. Shepley La. B60: Lick E ...4G 19
Lowes Cl. B61: B'gve ...5D 18
LOWES HILL ...5D 18
Loweswater Rd. DY13: Stour S ...5G 9
Low Field La. B97: Redd ...3D 26
LOW HABBERLEY ...5G 11
LOW HILL ...5G 11
Lowlands La. B98: Redd ...5D 28
Loxley Cl. B98: Redd ...2D 28
Luckett Cl. DY9: Hag ...3G 17
Lucy Baldwin Cl. DY13: Stour S ...1H 13
LUCY BALDWIN UNIT ...5C 6
 (WITHIN KIDDERMINSTER HOSPITAL)

Lucy Edwards Ct. DY11: Kidd ...5C 6
Ludgate Av. DY11: Kidd ...5A 6
Ludlow Rd. B97: Redd ...5F 27
 DY10: Kidd ...1E 11
Lupton Cl. B60: B'gve ...3D 22
Lydham Cl. B98: Redd ...3G 27
Lydney Cl. B98: Redd ...1D 28
Lygon Cl. WR9: Droit S ...3A 28
Lynden Cl. B61: B'gve ...1B 22
Lyndenwood B97: Redd ...6C 26
Lyndholm Rd. DY10: Kidd ...4G 7
Lyndhurst Dr. DY10: Kidd ...2E 7
Lynwood Dr. DY10: Blak ...6A 16
Lyttelton Cl. WR9: Droit S ...4F 25
Lyttelton Pl. DY9: Hag ...2H 17
Lyttelton Rd. WR9: Droit S ...5E 25
Lyttleton Av. B60: B'gve ...5B 22
Lyttleton Gro. B60: B'gve ...5C 22
Lyttleton Rd. DY12: Bew ...6C 4

M

Mabey Av. B98: Redd ...3H 27
Macarthur Way DY13: Stour S ...2A 14
McConnell Cl. B60: B'gve ...5E 23
Madeley Rd. B98: Redd ...3F 29
Magistrates' Court
 Bromsgrove & Redditch ...4G 27
 Kidderminster ...5F 7
Magpie Way DY10: Kidd ...2H 11
Maiden Way B60: B'gve ...6D 22
Mainstone Cl. B98: Redd ...5E 29
Maisemore Cl. B98: Redd ...1D 28
Malcolm Av. B61: B'gve ...1B 22
Malfield Av. B97: Redd ...5B 26
Malham Rd. DY13: Stour S ...5G 9
Malins, The B49: Alc ...4B 36
Mallard Av. DY10: Kidd ...1H 11
Mallard Cl. B98: Redd ...3H 27
Mallard Pl. WR9: Droit S ...3G 25
Mallard Rd. B80: Stud ...6F 33
Mallory Dr. DY11: Kidd ...1D 6
Mallow Cres. DY10: Kidd ...6F 7
Mallow Dr. B61: B'gve ...5C 18
Malt Ho. Wlk. WR9: Droit S ...1D 8
 (off Load St.)
Maltings, The B80: Stud ...6D 32
Malt Mill La. B49: Alc ...5C 36
Malvern Cl. DY13: Stour S ...5F 13
Malvern Dr. DY10: Kidd ...1E 11
Malvern Edge Ct. DY13: Stour S ...6G 13
Malvern Gdns. DY8: Hag ...3E 17
Malvern Ho. DY11: Kidd ...1E 31
Malvern Rd.
 B61: B'gve ...5A 22
 B97: Redd ...2F 31
Malvern Vw. DY11: Kidd ...3B 10
Mandarin Av. DY10: Kidd ...1H 11
Manders Cl. B96: A'wd B ...3A 34
Mandeville Way B61: B'gve ...5D 18
Manning Rd. WR9: Droit S ...4D 24
Manor Av. DY11: Kidd ...3A 6
 DY13: Stour S ...3A 6
Manor Cl. DY11: Kidd ...4A 6
 DY13: Stour S ...1B 14
 B97: Redd ...3F 25
Manor Ct. Rd. B60: B'gve ...4B 22
Manor Ho. La. B96: A'wd B ...1A 34
Manor La. DY11: Ware ...6G 15
Manor M. B80: Stud ...6E 33
Manor Rd. B80: Stud ...6E 33
 DY13: Stour S ...1A 14
Manor Side Ind. Est. B98: Redd ...2E 29
Manse Gdns. B80: Stud ...6E 33
Mansell Rd. B97: Redd ...3F 31
Maple Cl. DY11: Kidd ...2B 6
 DY13: Stour S ...2G 13
Maple Gro. WR9: Droit S ...6E 25
Maple Ho. B60: B'gve ...1D 22
 B98: Redd ...2H 31
 (off Alder Carr Cl.)
Mapplebrough Cl. B97: Redd ...3D 26
MAPPLEBOROUGH GREEN ...2D 33
Mapson Ct. WR9: Hag ...4H 25
Marble All. B80: Stud ...6E 33
March Gro. DY12: Bew ...6D 4
Marchwood Cl. B97: Redd ...3C 26
Margaret Llewelyn Davies Cl. B98: Redd ...5A 28
Margesson Dr. B45: B Grn ...1E 21
Marhon Cl. B98: Redd ...5C 25
Marina Point DY13: Stour S ...5G 13
Mark Cl. B98: Redd ...6G 27
Marketing Institute, The B80: Stud ...5H 33
Market Pl. B49: Alc ...5B 36
 B61: B'gve ...2G 22
 B98: Redd ...4G 27
Market St. B61: B'gve ...2C 22
 DY10: Kidd ...5E 7
Market Wlk. B97: Redd ...5E 7
 (off Kingfisher Shop. Cen.)
Marlbank Way DY9: Hag ...2H 17
Marlborough Av. B60: B'gve ...5D 22
Marlborough Cl. B60: B'gve ...4E 23
Marlborough Dr. DY13: Stour S ...6G 13
Marlborough M. B80: Stud ...6E 33
Marlborough St. DY10: Kidd ...5E 7

Marlbrook Gdns.—Northleach Cl.

Marlbrook Gdns. B61: Cats 1E **19**
Marlbrook La. B60: Marlb 1G **19**
Marlfield La. B98: Redd 4B **28**
(not continuous)
Marlgrove Ct. B61: Lick E 2F **19**
Marlowe Cl. DY10: Kidd 4H **7**
Marlpit La. B97: Redd 1D **30**
(not continuous)
Marlpool Cl. DY11: Kidd 1B **6**
Marlpool Ct. DY11: Kidd 2C **6**
Marlpool Dr. B97: Redd 5E **27**
Marlpool La. DY11: Kidd 1C **6**
Marlpool Pl. DY11: Kidd 2B **6**
Marsden Rd. B98: Redd 5G **27**
Marshfield Cl. B98: Redd 1B **28**
Marsh Gro. DY10: Kidd 2E **7**
Marsh Way B61: Cats 1C **18**
Martin Cl. B61: B'gve 3B **22**
Martingale Cl. B60: B'gve 6B **22**
Martins Way DY13: Stour S 3H **13**
Mart La. DY13: Stour S 3A **14**
Martley Cl. B98: Redd 3B **32**
Martley Rd. DY13: Stour S 6F **13**
Mary Windsor Ho. B60: B'gve 3C **22**
Masefield Gdns. DY10: Kidd 4H **7**
Mason Cl. B97: Redd 3F **31**
Mason Rd. B97: Redd 3F **31**
DY11: Kidd 4C **6**
MATCHBOROUGH 1E **33**
Matchborough Cen. B98: Redd 1E **33**
Matchborough Way B98: Redd 3E **33**
Matthew La. DY11: Kidd 3F **11**
Maund Cl. B60: B'gve 5B **22**
Maureen Aston Ct. *DY10: Kidd* *3E 7*
(off Broad St.)
Maurice Cl. DY9: Hag 3G **17**
Maxstoke Cl. B98: Redd 1D **32**
Mayberry Cl. DY13: Stour S 2G **13**
Mayfield Cl. B61: Cats 1C **18**
DY11: Kidd 2A **6**
Mayfields B98: Redd 6F **27**
Mayfields Gdns. B98: Redd 6F **27**
Mayflower Cl. DY13: Stour S 4A **14**
Mayflower Rd. WR9: Droit S 4F **25**
Maypole Cl. DY12: Bew 1E **9**
Maytree Hill WR9: Droit S 6F **25**
Meadow Cvn. Pk. DY13: Stour S 5B **14**
Meadow Cl. WR9: Droit S 2C **24**
Meadow Ct. WR9: Droit S 1C **24**
Meadowcroft DY9: Hag 4E **17**
Meadow Grn. WR9: Droit S 1C **24**
Meadow Hill Cl. DY11: Kidd 5A **6**
Meadowhill Cres. B98: Redd 3H **27**
Meadowhill Rd. B98: Redd 3H **27**
Meadow La. B48: A'chu 1H **21**
Meadow Mill Ind. Est. DY10: Kidd 5E **7**
Meadow Piece WR9: Droit S 1C **24**
Meadow Pl. WR9: Droit S 1C **24**
Meadow Rise DY12: Bew 6E **5**
Meadow Rd. B49: Alc 3B **36**
B61: Cats 2C **18**
WR9: Droit S 2C **24**
Meadows, The B61: Cats 2C **18**
DY9: Pedm 1G **17**
Meadowsweet Pl. *DY10: Kidd* *2D 6*
(off Alder Av.)
Meadow Va. DY13: Stour S 2B **14**
Meadowvale Rd. B60: Lick E 4F **19**
Meadow Vw. DY13: Stour S 6G **13**
Meadow Vw. Cl. B49: Alc 4C **36**
Meadow Vw. Ct. B80: Stud 1G **35**
Meadow Wlk. WR9: Droit S 2C **24**
Meadow Way WR9: Droit S 1C **24**
Meadway, The B97: Redd 1E **31**
Mearse La. B45: B Grn 2A **20**
Medici Rd. B60: B'gve 2F **23**
Meeting La. B49: Alc 4C **36**
Meir Rd. B98: Redd 2C **32**
Melbourne Av. B61: B'gve 6B **18**
Melbourne Cl. B61: B'gve 1B **22**
Melbourne Rd. B61: B'gve 6B **18**
Melbury Way B98: Redd 2D **28**
Melen St. B97: Redd 4F **27**
Mendip Cl. B61: B'gve 5D **18**
Mendip Ho. B98: Redd 2D **28**
Menteith Cl. DY13: Stour S 5G **9**
Mercia Cl. B60: B'gve 5C **22**
Mercot Cl. B98: Redd 4A **32**
Meredith Grn. DY11: Kidd 3A **10**
Merevale Cl. B98: Redd 2D **32**
Merganser Way DY10: Kidd 2H **11**
Meriden Cl. B98: Redd 5G **29**
Meridian Pl. B60: B'gve 2D **22**
Merlin Dr. DY10: Kidd 1H **11**
Merricks Cl. DY12: Bew 1B **8**
Merricks La. DY12: Bew 1B **8**
Merriemont Dr. B45: B Grn 1B **20**
Merrill Gdns. B60: Marlb 1G **19**
Merse Rd. B98: Redd 2E **29**
Merton Cl. DY10: Kidd 3G **7**
DY12: Bew 6B **4**
Michaelwood Cl. B97: Redd 6B **26**
Mickleton Cl. B98: Redd 3G **31**
Middlefield La. DY9: Hag 2G **17**
Middlefield Rd. B60: B'gve 5E **23**
Middle Ho. Dr. B60: Marlb 1G **19**
Middlehouse La. B97: Redd 2G **27**
Middle La. WR9: Droit S, Had 6G **25**
Middlemore Cl. B80: Stud 1F **35**
Middle Piece Dr. B97: Redd 6C **26**
Middleton Cl. B98: Redd 6F **29**
Middleton M. B98: Redd 6F **29**
Middleton Rd. B61: B'gve 6C **18**
DY11: Kidd 1C **6**
MIDDLETOWN 3F **35**
Middletown B80: Stud 3F **35**
Middletown La. B80: Stud 4E **35**
B96: Sam 4E **35**
Mikado Rd. B60: B'gve 3G **23**
Mike Oborski Cl. DY10: Kidd 4H **7**
Milcote Cl. B98: Redd 3H **31**
Milestone Dr. DY9: Hag 4E **17**
Milford Av. DY13: Stour S 6G **9**
Milford Cl. B97: Redd 3D **30**
Milhill Rd. B98: Redd 1E **33**
Mill Bank Ct. DY11: Kidd 4D **6**
Mill Cl. B60: B'gve 6C **22**
DY10: Blak 6A **16**
DY13: Stour S 3B **14**
Mill Ct. B48: A'chu 1H **21**
Milldale Cl. DY10: Kidd 2E **7**
Miller Cl. B60: B'gve 6B **22**
Miller St. WR9: Droit S 3E **25**
Millfield Gdns. DY11: Kidd 4D **6**
Millfield Rd. B61: B'gve 3A **22**
Millfields Ct. DY13: Stour S 2C **14**
Millfields Dr. DY13: Stour S 3B **14**
Millgate Cl. DY13: Stour S 2B **14**
Milligans Point *DY11: Kidd* *4D 6*
(off Mill La.)
Mill Ind. Pk., The B49: King C 1A **36**
Mill La. B49: Ove G 6B **36**
B61: B'gve 2C **22**
DY10: Blak 6A **16**
DY10: Kidd 2F **11**
DY11: Kidd 4D **6**
DY13: Stour S 2B **14**
Mill Pleck B80: Stud 1G **35**
Millpool Cl. DY9: Hag 4F **17**
Millrace Rd. B98: Redd 2G **27**
Millridge Way DY11: Hartl 5F **15**
Mill Rd. DY13: Stour S 2B **14**
Millsborough Rd. B98: Redd 5G **27**
(not continuous)
Millside Ct. DY12: Bew 1D **8**
Mill St. B97: Redd 4F **27**
DY11: Kidd 3C **6**
Milton Cl. B97: Redd 2E **31**
DY11: Kidd 4A **6**
Milton Dr. DY9: Hag 1H **17**
Milton Rd. B61: Cats 2D **18**
Milward Sq. *B97: Redd* *5G 27*
(off Kingfisher Shop. Cen.)
Minerva M. B49: Alc 4B **36**
Minerva Mill Innovation Cen. B49: Alc 4A **36**
Minerva Mill Technology Cen. *B49: Alc* *4B 36*
(off Station Rd.)
MINOR INJURIES UNIT (BROMSGROVE) 6D **18**
MINOR INJURIES UNIT (KIDDERMINSTER) 5C **6**
Minster Ct. DY13: Stour S 2A **14**
Minster Rd. DY13: Stour S 2A **14**
Minster Wlk. B61: Cats 2C **18**
Minter Av. WR9: Droit S 4D **24**
Minton M. B60: B'gve 4E **23**
Minworth Cl. B97: Redd 6D **26**
Mitcheldean Cl. B98: Redd 3G **31**
Mitre Ct. *B61: B'gve* *1D 22*
(off The Strand)
Mitton Cl. DY13: Stour S 2A **14**
Mitton Ct. DY13: Stour S 2B **14**
Mitton Gdns. DY13: Stour S 3A **14**
Mitton Lodge DY13: Stour S 2A **14**
Mitton Mill Ind. Est. DY13: Stour S 2C **14**
Mitton St. DY13: Stour S 3A **14**
Mitton Wlk. DY13: Stour S 3A **14**
MJM Golf Driving Range 6C **32**
Moat Ho. Ct. B80: Map G 2F **33**
Moat Mill La. B61: B'gve 3C **22**
Moffit Way DY13: Stour S 2G **13**
Monastery Av. DY10: Kidd 1F **7**
Mondrian Rd. B60: B'gve 3F **23**
Monks Dr. B80: Stud 6D **32**
Monks Path B97: Redd 4B **26**
Monnow Cl. WR9: Droit S 6D **24**
Montgomery Cl. B61: Cats 1D **18**
Monument La. DY9: Hag 1H **17**
MOONS MOAT 3E **29**
Moons Moat Dr. B98: Redd 3D **28**
Moons Pk. B98: Redd 2E **29**
Moorcroft Cl. B97: Redd 4D **30**
Moorcroft Gdns. B97: Redd 4D **30**
Moorfield Dr. B61: B'gve 1C **22**
Moorfield Rd. B49: Alc 5B **36**
(not continuous)
Moorgate Cl. B98: Redd 2E **29**
Moor Hall Dr. DY13: Stour S 2H **13**
Moorhall La. DY13: Stour S 2G **13**
MOORS, THE 4B **36**
Moors Av. DY11: Hartl 4H **15**
Moorsom Way B60: B'gve 5E **23**
Mordiford Cl. B98: Redd 5E **29**
Moreland Rd. WR9: Droit S 4D **24**
Morella Cl. DY12: Bew 1B **8**
Morgan Cl. B80: Stud 2G **35**
Morgan Dr. DY13: Stour S 1G **13**
Morillon Ct. DY10: Kidd 3G **11**
Morris Wlk. B60: B'gve 4B **22**
Morsefield La. B98: Redd 1D **32**
Mortimer Gro. DY12: Bew 6D **4**
Morton Ho. B97: Redd 5C **26**
Morton La. B97: Redd 4D **30**
Mosel Dr. WR9: Droit S 6C **24**
Moss La. B98: Beo 1F **29**
Mostyn Rd. DY13: Stour S 6G **9**
Moule Cl. DY11: Kidd 4B **6**
Mt. Pleasant B97: Redd 6F **27**
Mount Rd. B61: F'fld 1A **18**
Mountserrat Rd. B60: B'gve 3E **23**
Mount St. B98: Redd 5G **27**
Mt. Vernon Dr. B61: B'gve 5D **18**
Mouse La. DY11: Kidd 2B **6**
Mulberry Gro. B61: Cats 2E **19**
Mulberry Tree Hill WR9: Droit S 6F **25**
Munro Cl. DY10: Kidd 4H **7**
Munsley Cl. B98: Redd 6F **29**
Museum of Carpet 5E **7**
Musketts Ct. B97: Redd 6D **26**
Musketts Way B97: Redd 6E **27**
Muskoka DY12: Bew 1B **8**
Myrtle Av. B98: Redd 6G **27**

N

Nailers Cl. B60: Stoke H 6B **22**
Nailers Ct. B60: B'gve 2C **22**
Nailsworth Rd. B98: Redd 6H **27**
Nairn Cl. B98: Redd 4E **29**
Napton Cl. B98: Redd 1D **32**
Naseby Cl. B98: Redd 2D **28**
Nash Cl. DY10: Kidd 5H **7**
Nash Rd. B98: Redd 2B **32**
Naylor Cl. DY11: Kidd 1B **10**
Needle Cl. B80: Stud 6E **33**
Needle Ct. B97: Redd 5E **27**
Needle Mill La. B98: Redd 2G **27**
Needles Ho. B80: Stud 5E **33**
Neighbrook Cl. B97: Redd 6B **26**
Nelson Rd. DY13: Stour S 6B **14**
Nelson Tuery B49: Alc 5B **36**
Netherfield B98: Redd 2A **32**
Netherton La. DY12: Bew 2E **9**
DY13: Dunl 6A **12**
NETHERWICH 2E **25**
Netherwich Gdns. WR9: Droit S 2D **24**
Neville Av. DY11: Kidd 1D **10**
Neville Cl. B98: Redd 3H **27**
Neville Ct. DY11: Kidd 1D **10**
New Bldgs. DY11: Kidd 4D **6**
Newbury Cl. B61: Cats 1E **19**
New Chawson La. WR9: Droit S 5B **24**
New Coppice Ct. B97: Redd 4G **31**
Newent Cl. B98: Redd 5G **29**
Newfield Gdns. DY9: Hag 4F **17**
Newfield Pl. DY9: Hag 4F **17**
Newfield Rd. DY9: Hag 4F **17**
Newland Cl. B98: Redd 3B **32**
Newland Dr. WR9: Droit S 5E **25**
Newland Rd. WR9: Droit S 5E **25**
WR9: Newl 6F **25**
Newlands, The B80: Stud 1F **35**
Newlands Cl. DY9: Hag 2H **17**
DY11: Kidd 3C **6**
New Meadow Rd. B98: Redd 5B **28**
Newport Cl. B97: Redd 4D **30**
Newport Dr. B49: Alc 5B **36**
New Rd. B60: B'gve 2C **22**
B61: B'gve 1B **22**
B61: F'fld 1B **18**
B80: Stud 6E **33**
B96: A'wd B 4A **34**
DY10: Kidd 6E **7**
DY12: Bew 5F **5**
New St. DY13: Stour S 3H **13**
Newton Cl. B98: Redd 4A **32**
DY12: Bew 6B **4**
Newton Rd. B60: B'gve 5D **22**
Newton Sq. B60: B'gve 5D **22**
NEWTOWN 3C **24**
New Wlk. *B97: Redd* *4G 27*
(off Kingfisher Shop. Cen.)
Nightingale Cl. WR9: Droit S 6G **25**
Nightingale Dr. DY10: Kidd 2H **11**
Nina Cl. DY13: Stour S 3B **14**
Nine Days La. B98: Redd 4B **32**
Nine Foot Way WR9: Droit S 3E **25**
Node Hill B80: Stud 1F **35**
Node Hill Cl. B80: Stud 1F **35**
Noel Ct. B97: Redd 2E **31**
Noonan Cl. B97: Redd 6D **26**
Norbury Cl. B98: Redd 1B **28**
Norbury Ho. *WR9: Droit S* *3E 25*
(off Friar St.)
Norbury Theatre & Cinema 3E **25**
Norgrove La. B97: Elc B, Up Ben 4A **30**
Norman Broome Ct. DY11: Kidd 5D **6**
Norris Cl. B60: B'gve 5F **23**
Northcliffe Hgts. DY11: Kidd 3C **6**
Northfield Cl. B98: Redd 2D **28**
Northgate Cl. DY11: Kidd 6A **6**
Northleach Cl. B98: Redd 3B **28**

Nth. Moons Moat Ind. Area B98: Redd 3E 29
North Rd. B60: B'gve 2D 22
  DY13: Stour S 1A 14
Northside Cl. B98: Redd 3G 31
North St. WR9: Droit S 3D 24
North St. Ind. Est. WR9: Droit S 3D 24
Northumberland Av. DY11: Kidd 1G 10
Northwood Halt Station
  Severn Valley Railway 3B 4
Northwood La. DY12: Bew 3B 4
Norton Cl. B98: Redd 6F 29
Norton M. B61: B'gve 6E 19
Norton Rd. DY10: Kidd .4H 7
Norwich Av. DY11: Kidd 4H 5
Nuffield Dr. WR9: Droit S 3B 24
Nunnery Av. WR9: Droit S 4D 24
Nursery Cl. DY9: Hag 4F 17
  DY11: Kidd 2B 6
Nursery Gro. DY11: Kidd 2B 6
Nursery Rd. DY12: Bew 6D 4

O

Oakalls Av. B60: B'gve .2E 23
Oak Apple Cl. DY13: Stour S 6G 13
Oak Apple Ct. B61: Cats 2E 19
Oak Apple Rd. B61: Cats 2E 19
Oakdene DY13: Stour S 3B 14
Oakdene Dr. B45: B Grn 2D 20
Oakden Pl. DY11: Kidd .3C 6
OAKENSHAW 4G 31
Oakenshaw Rd. B98: Redd 2H 31
Oakfield Rd. DY11: Kidd 5B 6
Oak Gro. DY10: Kidd 5G 7
Oakham Cl. B98: Redd .5A 32
Oakham Dr. WR9: Droit S 4B 24
Oakham Grn. WR9: Droit S 4B 24
                          (off Little Hill)
Oakham Pl. WR9: Droit S 4C 24
Oakhampton Rd. DY13: Stour S 6G 13
Oakhill Av. DY10: Kidd .6E 7
Oakhurst Dr. B60: B'gve 1D 22
Oakland Av. WR9: Droit S 5D 24
Oakland Gro. B61: B'gve 6E 19
Oaklands, The DY10: Kidd 3G 7
  WR9: Droit S 5D 24
Oaklands Bus. Pk. DY11: Kidd 3E 11
Oaklands Cl. B61: Stoke H 6A 22
Oakleigh Rd. WR9: Droit S 5B 24
Oakley Ho. B60: B'gve .2D 22
Oakly Rd. B97: Redd 5F 27
Oakridge Cl. B98: Redd 1C 28
Oak Rd. B61: Cats 2E 19
Oaks Ct. B98: Redd 1C 28
Oak Tree Av. B97: Redd 4D 26
Oak Tree La. B48: A'chu 3H 21
Oak Tree La. B96: Sam .2D 34
Oak Tree Pk. B98: Redd 2F 29
Oakwood Rd. DY12: Bew 1B 8
Oasis, The DY9: Hag 3E 17
Oasthouse Cl. B60: Stoke H 6A 22
Oatfields WR9: Droit S .2A 24
Offenham Cl. B98: Redd 2B 28
OFFMORE FARM 4G 7
Offmore Farm Cl. DY10: Kidd 4H 7
Offmore La. DY10: Kidd 4G 7
Offmore Rd. DY10: Kidd 4F 7
Offwell Cl. B98: Redd 1D 32
Old Bakery Ct. DY9: Hag 3F 17
Old Birmingham Rd.
  B60: Lick E, Marlb 3F 19
Oldbury Cl. B98: Redd .2B 28
Old Chawson La. WR9: Droit S 5B 24
Old Chester Rd. Sth. DY10: Kidd 2F 11
Old Coach Rd. WR9: Droit S 4D 24
Old Crest Av. B98: Redd 5G 27
Oldfield Rd. B61: B'gve .5B 18
Oldfields DY9: Hag 2G 23
Old Ford Wlk. DY13: Stour S 6G 13
Old Forge Bus. Cen. B98: Redd 2C 32
Old Forge Dr. B98: Redd 1C 32
Old Forge Gdns. DY11: Hartl 4H 15
Oldington Driving Range 5B 10
Oldington La. DY11: Kidd 4B 10
Oldington Trad. Est. DY11: Kidd 3B 10
Oldnall Rd. DY10: Kidd .6F 7
Old Rectory Gdn. B49: Alc 4B 36
Old Rectory La. B48: A'chu 3H 21
Old Station Rd. B60: B'gve 3C 22
                           (Ednall La.)
  B60: B'gve 2F 23
                    (Stonehouse Rd.)
Old Stratford Rd. B60: B'gve 2F 23
Old Tannery Ct. DY12: Bew 1D 8
Old Vicarage Gdns. B80: Stud 6E 33
Old Worcester Rd. DY11: Hartl, Ware 5G 15
Olive Gro. DY13: Stour S 2H 13
Olympian Ct. DY10: Kidd 3E 7
Olympus Gdns. DY13: Stour S 3C 14
Ombersley Cl. B98: Redd 3B 32
  WR9: Droit S 3D 24
Ombersley Rd. WR9: Droit S 3D 24
Ombersley St. WR9: Droit S 3D 24
Ombersley St. E. WR9: Droit S 3E 25
Ombersley St. W. WR9: Droit S 3D 24
Ombersley Way WR9: Droit S 4B 24

Orchard, The B61: B'gve 6B 18
  B96: A'wd B 1A 8
Orchard Cl. DY9: Hag 4G 17
  DY13: Stour S 2B 14
Orchard Cft. B45: B Grn 2E 21
Orchard Dr. B49: Alc 6B 36
Orchard Gro. B96: A'wd B 5A 34
Orchard Lea WR9: Droit S 5F 11
Orchard Pl. B80: Map G 2F 33
Orchard Ri. DY12: Bew .1C 8
  WR9: Droit S 6D 24
Orchard Rd. B61: B'gve 6C 18
Orchards, The B96: A'wd B 3A 34
  DY11: Kidd 1B 6
Orchard St. B98: Redd .5G 27
  DY10: Kidd 4E 7
Orchard Way B80: Stud 2G 35
Oriole Gro. DY10: Kidd .2H 11
Orion Pl. DY13: Stour S 3H 13
Osborne Cl. DY10: Kidd .4H 7
Osborne Rd. B60: B'gve 3F 23
Osier Cl. B61: B'gve 2B 22
Osiers, The DY13: Stour S 2C 14
Osnor Ct. B60: B'gve 5E 23
Osprey Ho. B80: Stud 6D 32
Osprey Pk. Dr. DY10: Kidd 1H 11
Oswald St. B98: Redd .5G 27
Oswestry Cl. B97: Redd .3E 31
Other Rd. B98: Redd 4G 27
                       (not continuous)
Otter Cl. B98: Redd 5F 29
Oulton Cl. DY11: Kidd 2D 6
Outwood Cl. B98: Redd 3G 31
Overdale B96: A'wd B 3A 34
Oversley Cl. B97: Redd .2E 27
OVERSLEY GREEN 6C 36
Oversley Ho. B49: Alc 4C 36
Oversley Mill Pk. B49: Ove G 6B 36
Ox Bow Way DY10: Kidd 2E 7
Oxford St. DY10: Kidd 4E 7
Oxhill Cl. B98: Redd 1E 33
Oxleasow Rd. B98: Redd 4E 29

P

Packington Rd. WR9: Droit S 4D 24
Packwood Cl. B97: Redd 1B 30
Padbury Cl. B98: Redd .1C 28
Paddock, The B60: Stoke H 6A 22
  DY13: Stour S 6F 9
Paddock Cl. WR9: Droit S 1B 24
Paddock Grn. WR9: Droit S 1C 24
                     (off Paddock Way)
Paddock Hill WR9: Droit S 1C 24
                     (off Paddock Way)
Paddock La. B98: Redd .3G 31
Paddock Way WR9: Droit S 1C 24
Padgets La. B98: Redd .4D 28
Padgewell Hill WR9: Droit S 4C 24
Padua Rd. B60: B'gve 3F 23
Paget Cl. B61: B'gve 2B 22
Painswick Cl. B98: Redd 4G 31
Palace Theatre
  Redditch 4G 27
Palmers Rd. B98: Redd .3F 29
Palmyra Rd. B60: B'gve .2F 23
Pannier Cl. DY10: Kidd .5F 7
Paper Mill Dr. B98: Redd 3B 28
Papworth Dr. B61: B'gve 5C 18
Parade, The DY10: Kidd .2F 7
Parade Ct. B80: Stud 6E 33
Paradise Row B60: B'gve 2C 22
Parish Hill B61: Bourn .1A 18
Park, The DY12: Bew 1D 8
Park All. DY12: Bew 1D 8
Park Av. B80: Stud 1G 35
  DY13: Stour S 2H 13
Park Butts Ringway DY11: Kidd 4D 6
Park Cl. DY12: Bew 1C 8
Park Ct. B98: Redd 5A 28
Park Cres. DY13: Stour S 2H 13
Park Dingle DY12: Bew .4A 8
PARK END 5C 10
Parker Pl. DY11: Kidd 5C 10
Parkes Pas. DY13: Stour S 3A 14
Parkes Quay DY13: Stour S 3A 14
PARK FARM 2B 32
Park Farm Ind. Est. B98: Redd 3C 32
                     (Lit. Forge Rd.)
  B98: Redd 3D 32
                       (Pipers Rd.)
PARK FARM SOUTH 4D 32
Parkfield Cl. B98: Redd .2B 28
  DY11: Hartl 4G 15
Parkland Av. DY11: Kidd 5B 6
Parklands, The WR9: Droit S 5E 25
Parklands Cl. B97: Redd 3C 26
Park La. DY11: Kidd 4D 6
  DY12: Bew 2B 8
Park La. Ind. Est. DY11: Kidd 6D 6
Park Ri. DY11: Kidd 5D 6
Park Rd. DY9: Hag 3F 17
Parkside B61: B'gve 1D 22
Parkstone Av. B61: B'gve 4A 22
Park St. DY11: Kidd 4D 6
Park St. Gdns. DY11: Kidd 4D 6

Park Vw. B49: Arr 6A 36
Park Wlk. B97: Redd 5G 27
                (off Kingfisher Shop. Cen.)
Park Way B98: Redd 3A 28
  WR9: Droit S 2C 24
Parkwood Ct. DY11: Kidd 4D 6
                       (off Park St.)
Parliament Pl. B61: B'gve 1B 22
Parmington Cl. B97: Redd 4D 30
Parry Rd. DY11: Kidd 1B 10
Parsonage Ct. B61: B'gve 5B 18
                       (off Blakeney Dr.)
Parsons Cnr. WR9: Droit S 5C 24
                    (off Padgewell Hill)
Parsons Ct. DY13: Stour S 2B 14
Parsons La. DY11: Hartl .6F 15
  DY13: C'wick 6F 15
Parsons Rd. B98: Redd .6G 27
Partridge Gro. DY10: Kidd 2G 11
Partridge Ho. B97: Redd 6F 27
                      (off Mt. Pleasant)
Partridge La. B97: Redd .4C 30
Partridge Retail Pk. WR9: Droit S 1D 24
Pastorale Rd. B60: B'gve 3F 23
Patchetts La. DY12: Bew 6C 4
Patch La. B98: Redd 4H 31
Pat Davis Ct. DY10: Kidd 3E 7
Paternoster Row DY11: Kidd 4D 6
Patios, The DY11: Kidd .3C 6
Pavilion Gdns. B61: B'gve 5C 18
Paxford Cl. B98: Redd 2B 28
Paxton Cl. B60: B'gve 3E 23
Peacock M. WR9: Droit S 2E 7
Peakman St. B98: Redd .4G 27
Pearl La. DY13: Stour S .5F 13
Pearl Dr. B80: Stud 6D 32
Pear Tree Cl. DY10: Kidd 3H 7
Pebworth Cl. B98: Redd 1C 28
Pedmore Cl. B98: Redd .3B 32
Peel St. DY11: Kidd 5D 6
Pelham Lodge DY10: Kidd 5F 7
Pelham Rd. WR9: Droit S 6D 24
Peltland Trad. Cen. B98: Redd 4D 28
Pembridge Cl. B98: Redd 5D 28
Pembroke Way DY13: Stour S 6G 9
Pendine Cl. DY11: Kidd .1D 6
Penmanor B60: Fins 5H 23
Pennine Rd. B61: B'gve .5D 18
Pennyford Cl. B97: Redd 3C 26
Penrice Rd. WR9: Droit S 5D 24
Penshurst Rd. B60: B'gve 3F 23
Penzer Dr. B45: B Grn 2D 20
Percheron Way WR9: Droit S 6G 25
Peregrine Gro. DY10: Kidd 2G 11
Perrett Wlk. DY11: Kidd .4D 6
Perrin Av. DY11: Kidd 4D 6
PERRYFIELDS 1A 22
Perryfields Cl. B98: Redd 5H 31
Perryfields Cres. B'gve .5C 18
Perryfields Rd. B61: B'gve 1A 22
Perry La. B61: B'gve 2C 22
  DY10: Tort 1H 15
Perrymill La. B96: Sam .3D 34
Pershore Rd. DY11: Kidd 4A 6
Peterbrook Cl. B98: Redd 3H 31
Petersfield Dr. WR9: Droit S 4G 25
Peter's Finger B61: B'gve 3C 22
Petton Cl. B98: Redd 5F 29
Pevensey Rd. B60: B'gve 3F 23
Pewterers All. DY12: Bew 6D 4
Pheasant Cl. DY10: Kidd 2G 11
Pheasant La. B98: Redd 5G 31
Phebe Bell Ct. B61: B'gve 1C 22
Phillips Ter. B98: Redd .4H 27
Phoenix Ho. DY11: Kidd 2B 6
Pike Hill B60: B'will 3B 20
                       (not continuous)
Pikes Pool La. B60: Burc, Fins 3G 23
Pilgrim Rd. WR9: Droit S 4G 25
Pinedene DY13: Stour S .3B 14
Pineridge Dr. DY11: Kidd 5B 6
Pine Rd. DY12: Bew 2B 8
Pine Wlk. DY13: Stour S .2G 13
Pinewood Cl. DY11: Kidd 1C 6
Pinewoods Av. DY9: Hag 4E 17
Pinewoods Cl. DY9: Hag 4E 17
Pinewoods Ct. DY9: Hag 4E 17
Pinfield Dr. B45: B Grn .1C 20
PINK GREEN 1H 29
Pink Grn. La. B97: Redd 3E 27
Pinnacle Ho. B97: Redd 5G 31
                      (off Evesham Rd.)
Pinta Dr. DY13: Stour S .3B 14
Pintail Gro. DY10: Kidd .1H 11
Pinvin Ho. B97: Redd 4C 26
Pioneer Cl. B97: Redd 4F 27
Pipe Cl. B98: Redd 5H 27
Pipers Cl. B61: B'gve 5H 7
Pipers Rd. B98: Redd 4D 32
Pipit Ct. DY10: Kidd 2G 11
Pitchcombe Cl. B98: Redd 5A 28
Pitcheroak Cotts. B97: Redd 7C 26
Pitcheroak Golf Course .6F 27
Pitts La. DY10: Kidd 4E 7
Pitt St. DY10: Kidd 1G 7

Plane Tree Cl. DY10: Kidd 3F 7
Planetree Cl. B60: B'gve 2E 23
Platform Rd. B60: B'gve 6E 23
Pleasant Harbour DY12: Bew 6D 4
Pleasant St. DY10: Kidd 3E 7
Plimsoll St. DY11: Kidd 5D 6
Ploughmans Ct. WR9: Droit S 1C 24
Ploughmans Piece WR9: Droit S 1C 24
(off Ploughmans Way)
Ploughmans Ri. WR9: Droit S 1C 24
Ploughmans Wlk. B60: Stoke H 6A 22
WR9: Droit S 1C 24
Ploughmans Way WR9: Droit S 1C 24
Plover Cl. B49: Alc .3B 36
Plover Gro. DY10: Kidd 3H 11
Plumstead Cl. B97: Redd 2D 26
Plymouth Cl. B97: Redd 6E 27
Plymouth Ct. B97: Redd 1E 31
Plymouth Dr. B45: B Grn 2B 20
Plymouth Rd. B45: B Grn 1B 20
B97: Redd .6F 27
Pochard Cl. DY10: Kidd 3F 11
Poets Ct. B61: Cats 2D 18
Polesworth Cl. B98: Redd 1D 32
Pool Bank B97: Redd 1F 31
B98: Redd .1F 31
Pooles Ct. DY10: Kidd 3E 7
Pool Pl. B98: Redd 5G 27
Pool Rd. B80: Stud 6E 33
Popes La. B96: A'wd B 2A 34
Popes Mdw. B96: A'wd B 1A 34
Poplar Cl. B49: Ove G 5D 36
B61: Cats .2C 18
Poplar Dr. B45: B Grn 2E 21
Poplar Rd. B97: Redd 5C 26
DY11: Kidd .6C 6
Poplar Row DY11: Kidd 6C 6
Poplars Trad. Est. B80: Stud 4D 32
Portland Rd. WR9: Droit S 5G 25
Post Office Wlk. B96: A'wd B 3A 34
Poverty B96: A'wd B 3A 34
Power Sta. Rd. DY13: Stour S 4A 14
Pratts La. B80: Map G 3F 33
Precision Way B49: Alc 2C 36
Prestbury Cl. B98: Redd 5G 29
Preston Cl. B98: Redd 2B 28
Price Cl. DY9: Hag 3G 17
Pridzor Cl. WR9: Droit S 2F 25
Pridzor Rd. WR9: Droit S 2F 25
Priestfield Rd. B97: Redd 5G 31
Priest Mdw. Cl. B96: A'wd B 3A 34
PRIMROSE AT THE PRINCESS (HOSPICE) 6D 18
Primrose Cl. B60: Lick E 4F 19
PRIMROSE HOSPICE 5F 23
Primrose La. B49: Ove G 6C 36
Primrose Way DY10: Kidd 6F 7
PRIMSLAND 6F 25
Primsland Dr. WR9: Droit S 5G 25
Primsland Flds. WR9: Droit S 6F 25
Primsland Way WR9: Droit S 6D 24
Prince M. DY9: Hag 1H 17
Prince Rupert Rd. DY13: Stour S 4G 13
Princes Av. WR9: Droit S 5E 25
PRINCESS OF WALES COMMUNITY HOSPITAL . .6D 18
Princess Way DY13: Stour S 5G 13
Prior Cl. DY10: Kidd 5H 7
Priors Oak B97: Redd 4D 26
Priory, The DY13: Stour S 1A 14
Priory Ct. B80: Stud 5E 33
Priory Gdns. WR9: Droit S 3E 25
Priory La. WR9: Droit S 3E 25
Priory Rd. B49: Alc 4B 36
Priory Sq. B80: Stud 5E 33
Priory Tuery B49: Alc 5B 36
Pritchard Cl. DY12: Bew 1D 8
Proctors Barn La. B98: Redd 4B 28
Prophet's Cl. B97: Redd 5F 27
Prospect Hill B97: Redd 4G 27
DY10: Kidd 4E 7
Prospect La. DY10: Kidd 4E 7
Prospect Rd. DY13: Stour S 2A 14
Prospect Rd. Nth. B98: Redd 4A 28
Prospect Rd. Sth. B98: Redd 4A 28
Prospect Ter. DY10: Kidd 4E 7
Proud Cross Ringway DY11: Kidd 4C 6
Providence Rd. B61: B'gve 1C 22
Prudden Cl. B97: Redd 4E 31
Puddlestone Cl. B96: A'wd B 4A 34
Pulley La. WR9: Cop, Newl 6A 24
Pullman Cl. DY13: Stour S 2A 14
Pulman Cl. B97: Redd 4E 27
Pumphouse La. B45: B Grn 2A 20
B60: B'wll 2A 20
B97: Redd, Up Ben 1A 30
Pump St. DY10: Kidd 6E 7
Purcell Ho. DY11: Kidd 4H 5
Purshall Cl. B97: Redd 5E 27
Purton Cl. B49: Alc 3C 36
Puxton Dr. DY11: Kidd 1D 6
Puxton La. DY11: Kidd 3C 6

Q

Quail Pk. Dr. DY10: Kidd 2G 11
Quantock Dr. DY10: Kidd 4G 7
Quarry, The DY10: Kidd 2F 7

Quarry Bank DY11: Hartl 4G 15
Quarry La. B61: B'gve 4A 22
Quayle Cl. DY11: Kidd 5C 6
Queen Elizabeth Rd. DY10: Kidd 4H 7
Queen's Cotts. B97: Redd 4D 26
Queen's Rd. DY13: Stour S 5H 13
Queen St. B96: A'wd B 3A 34
B98: Redd .4G 27
DY10: Kidd .3E 7
WR9: Droit S 3F 25
Queensway DY12: Bew 5E 5
Quibury Cl. B98: Redd 5F 29
Quinneys La. B98: Redd 4B 32
Quinton Cl. B98: Redd 1D 32

R

Radford Av. DY10: Kidd 3E 7
Radford Ho. B97: Redd 4C 26
Radford Rd. B48: A'chu 1H 21
Radway Cl. B98: Redd 2B 28
Raglan Ct. B60: B'gve 3D 22
Ragley Cres. B60: B'gve 4D 22
Ragley Mill La. B49: Alc 3B 36
Raglis Cl. B97: Redd 1C 30
Railway Cl. B80: Stud 6D 32
Railway M. B49: Alc 4B 36
Railway Wlk. B60: B'gve 6D 22
Rainsford Cres. DY10: Kidd 3D 6
Randall Av. B48: A'chu 4H 21
Rangeways Rd. DY11: Kidd 2A 6
Rangeworthy Cl. B97: Redd 3E 31
Rannoch Cl. DY13: Stour S 5G 9
Ravensbank Bus. Pk. B98: Redd 2C 28
Ravensbank Dr. B98: Redd 1C 28
Ravenscroft Dr. WR9: Droit S 4G 25
Ravensmere Rd. B98: Redd 1B 32
Raven St. DY13: Stour S 3H 13
Ray Mercer Way DY10: Kidd 5F 7
Rear Cotts. B48: A'chu 4G 21
Rebekah Gdns. WR9: Droit S 6E 25
Recreation Rd. B61: B'gve 1C 22
Rectory Ct. B97: Redd 1F 31
Rectory Gdns. DY11: Hartl 3G 15
Rectory La. DY11: Hartl 3G 15
DY13: Stour S 4F 13
Rectory Rd. B97: Redd 1F 31
Redcar Cl. B61: Cats 1E 19
RED CROSS 1A 22
REDDITCH 4G 27
Redditch Bus Station 5F 27
Redditch Crematorium B97: Redd 2G 27
Redditch Golf Cen. 2C 30
Redditch Ringway B97: Redd 4F 27
B98: Redd .4F 27
Redditch Rd. B48: A'chu, Redd 2H 21
B60: Stoke H 6A 22
B80: Stud .5D 32
Redditch Sailing Club 5B 28
Redditch Station (Rail) 4F 27
Redditch United FC 4E 27
Red Hill B98: Redd 6H 27
DY12: Bew .2D 8
Red Hill Cl. B80: Stud 4E 33
Redhouse Rd. DY13: Stour S 6F 13
Redlake Dr. DY9: Pedm 1G 17
Redland Cl. B60: Marlb 1F 19
Red Lion Ct. B96: A'wd B 2A 34
Red Lion St. B48: A'chu 1H 21
B98: Redd .4G 27
Red Pear Dr. B61: B'gve 6B 18
Redstart Av. DY10: Kidd 2H 11
Redstone Cvn. Pk. DY13: Stour S 5A 14
Redstone Cl. B98: Redd 2C 28
Redstone La. DY13: Stour S 6G 13
Redstone Marsh Local Nature Reserve 5H 13
Redwing Cl. DY10: Kidd 3G 11
Redwood Ho. B60: B'gve 1D 22
Reed Mace Dr. B61: B'gve 5D 18
Reel Cinema
Kidderminster 5E 7
Reeve Cl. DY10: Kidd 3G 11
Regal Gdns. B61: B'gve 4B 22
Regency Dr. B49: King C 2A 36
Regent Ct. B98: Redd 3F 29
Regent M. B61: B'gve 4B 22
Regents Pk. Rd. B60: B'gve 2E 23
Reitenbach Gro. DY9: Hag 3H 17
Renfrew Gdns. DY11: Kidd 5C 6
Renshaw Ind. Est. B80: Stud 6B 32
Reservoir Rd. DY11: Kidd 1C 10
Resolution Way DY13: Stour S 4B 14
Retreat, The B61: Lick E 4E 19
Retreat St. B96: A'wd B 3A 34
Reyde Cl. B97: Redd 6B 26
Reynard Cl. B97: Redd 5B 26
Rhuddlan Way DY10: Kidd 3E 11
RIBBESFORD 4C 8
Ribbesford Dr. DY13: Stour S 2G 13
Ribbesford Ho. DY12: Ribb 4D 8
Ribbesford Rd. DY12: Ribb 5D 8
DY13: Stour S 3E 13
Richmond Rd. DY12: Bew 1B 8
Rickets Cl. DY11: Kidd 5B 10
Rickett's La. WR9: Droit S 3E 25

Ricketts Pl. DY12: Bew 1D 8
Rickyard La. B98: Redd 3D 28
Riddell Cl. B49: Alc 4D 36
Riddings Cl. DY12: Bew 5E 5
Ridgeway, The B96: A'wd B 5A 34
DY13: Stour S 1H 13
WR9: Droit S 4G 25
Ridgeway Cl. B80: Stud 2G 35
Ridgeway Trad. Est. B96: A'wd B 2A 34
Ridings La. B98: Redd 1B 28
Rifle Range Rd. DY11: Kidd 1B 10
Rigby Hall B60: B'gve 4F 23
Rigby La. B60: B'gve 4E 23
Ringway, The DY10: Kidd 4E 7
Ripple Rd. WR9: Droit S 4D 24
River Arrow Nature Reserve 4B 36
RIVERSIDE 3H 27
Riverside B49: Alc .4D 36
B80: Stud .6E 33
Riverside Cvn. Pk. DY12: Bew 6C 4
Riverside Cl. B60: Lick E 4F 19
Riverside Ind. Est. B98: Redd 2C 32
Riverside Nth. DY12: Bew 6D 4
Riverside Way WR9: Droit S 3G 25
River Vw. DY13: Stour S 3A 14
Riverway Dr. DY12: Bew 6D 4
Road No. 1 DY10: Kidd 2E 11
Road No. 2 DY10: Kidd 2E 11
Road No. 3 DY10: Kidd 2E 11
Robeson Cl. WR9: Droit S 3G 25
Robin Ct. DY10: Kidd 2G 11
Robins Hill Dr. B48: A'chu 5H 21
Robins La. B97: Redd 2E 27
Robinson M. B98: Redd 2D 28
Rochester Cl. B97: Redd 2E 31
Rochester Wlk. DY10: Kidd 5H 7
Rockford Cl. B98: Redd 5H 31
ROCK HILL 5A 22
Rock Hill B61: B'gve 5A 22
Rockingham Hall Gdns. DY9: Hag 1H 17
Rocky La. B61: Bourn 3A 16
DY10: C'hll, Ism 3A 16
Roden Av. DY10: Kidd 3F 7
Roebuck Pk. B49: Alc 3A 36
Roman Alcester Mus. 5B 36
Roman Way B49: Alc 5B 36
B61: B'gve .6E 19
WR9: Droit S 4B 24
Roman Way Bus. Cen. WR9: Droit S 1D 24
Romsley Cl. B98: Redd 5F 29
Rookery, The B49: Alc 5C 36
(off Stratford Rd.)
Rookery Cl. B97: Redd 1F 31
Rooks Mdw. DY9: Hag 2G 17
Rope Wlk. DY12: Bew 1E 9
Ropewalk B49: Alc .4B 36
Rose Av. B48: A'chu 4H 21
DY13: Stour S 3G 25
Rose Cl. WR9: Droit S 3G 25
Rosedale Cl. B97: Redd 4C 26
Rose Dene DY13: Stour S 2G 13
Rosehall Cl. B98: Redd 4G 31
Rosemary Rd. DY10: Kidd 3H 7
Rosenhurst Dr. DY12: Bew 1C 8
Rose Ter. B45: B Grn 2E 21
Rosetti Cl. DY10: Kidd 4H 7
Rosewood Dr. B45: B Grn 3D 20
Roslin Cl. B60: B'gve 3E 23
Rough, The B97: Redd 2F 31
Rough Hill Dr. B98: Redd 5G 31
Rough Hill Wood (Nature Reserve) 5A 32
Round Hill Ct. DY10: Kidd 5D 6
Round Hill Wharf DY11: Kidd 5D 6
Rowanberry Cl. DY13: Stour S 2G 13
Rowan Cl. B61: B'gve 2B 22
DY10: Kidd .6E 25
Rowan Ct. WR9: Droit S 3E 25
Rowan Cres. B97: Redd 4C 26
Rowan Ho. DY11: Kidd 1B 6
Rowan Rd. B97: Redd 4C 26
Rowborough Cl. B96: A'wd B 2A 34
Rowland Av. B80: Stud 1G 35
Rowland Hill Av. DY11: Kidd 5B 6
Rowland Hill Cen. DY10: Kidd 4E 7
(off Josiah Mason Mall)
Rowland Hill Ho. DY10: Kidd 4E 7
Rowland Way DY11: Kidd 3E 11
Roxall Cl. DY10: Blak 6B 16
Roxborough Ho. B97: Redd 6F 27
Royal Sq. B97: Redd 5G 27
(off Kingfisher Shop. Cen.)
Royal Worcester Cres. B60: B'gve 3F 23
Rozel Av. DY10: Kidd 1H 7
Rufford Cl. B49: Alc 3C 36
Runcorn Cl. B98: Redd 2H 31
Rush La. B98: Redd 2B 28
Rushock Cl. B98: Redd 3C 32
Rushy Cl. WR9: Droit S 4D 24
Ruskin Av. DY10: Kidd 4H 7
Russel Cft. B60: B'gve 5D 22
Russell Rd. DY10: Kidd 6F 7
Russett Way DY12: Bew 6B 4
Ruth Chamberlain Ct. DY11: Kidd 4D 6
(off Paternoster Row)
Rutherford Rd. B60: B'gve 6E 23
Rutland Dr. B60: B'gve 4D 22

Rydal Cl. DY13: Stour S	6H 9
Rye Cl. WR9: Droit S	4F 25
Ryefield Cl. DY9: Hag	4F 17
Rye Grass La. B97: Redd	4E 31
Rye Lea, The WR9: Droit S	4C 24
(off Padgewell Hill)	
Ryknild St. B08: Rodd	1C 29
Ryland Ho. B97: Redd	4F 27
Ryton Cl. B98: Redd	1D 32
Ryvere Cl. DY13: Stour S	4H 13

S

Sabrina Dr. DY12: Bew	6C 4
Sacred Heart Church	5D 24
Sail Ho. DY13: Stour S	4A 14
St Agnes Cl. B80: Stud	6C 32
St Alban's Av. DY11: Kidd	3A 6
St Ambrose Pl. DY10: Kidd	4F 7
St Andrew's Cl. WR9: Droit S	3E 25
St Andrew's Dr. WR9: Droit S	4E 25
St Andrews Grn. DY10: Kidd	6E 7
St Andrew's Rd. WR9: Droit S	3E 25
St Andrews Sq. WR9: Droit S	3E 25
St Andrew's St. WR9: Droit S	3E 25
St Andrews Way B61: B'gve	4A 22
St Asaphs Av. B80: Stud	6D 32
St Augustine Dr. WR9: Droit S	2F 25
St Augustine's Cl. WR9: Droit S	2F 25
St Augustines Sports Cen.	5F 31
St Bartholomew's Rd. DY13: Stour S	4G 13
St Catherines Cl. B60: B'wll	5B 20
St Catherines Coppice B60: B'wll	4B 20
St Catherine's Rd. B60: B'wll	4A 20
St Cecilia Cl. DY10: Kidd	2E 11
St Chads Rd. B80: Stud	6C 32
St David's Cl. DY11: Kidd	4H 5
DY13: Stour S	6G 9
St David's Ho. B97: Redd	4D 26
St Faith's Rd. B49: Alc	3B 36
ST GEORGE'S	4H 27
St Georges Ct. B98: Redd	5E 29
DY10: Kidd	4F 7
St George's Cres. WR9: Droit S	3F 25
St Georges Gdns. B98: Redd	4H 27
St George's Pl. DY10: Kidd	3E 7
St George's Rd. B98: Redd	4H 27
St George's Sq. WR9: Droit S	3F 25
St George's Ter. DY10: Kidd	4F 7
St Godwald's Cres. B61: B'gve	4E 23
St Godwalds Rd. B60: B'gve	5E 23
St James Ct. B61: B'gve	1D 22
DY10: Blak	6A 16
St John's Av. DY11: Kidd	3A 6
St John's Cl. DY11: Kidd	4C 6
St John's Rd. DY13: Stour S	1A 14
St John's St. DY11: Kidd	4C 6
St John St. B61: B'gve	2C 22
St Joseph's Cl. WR9: Droit S	4C 24
St Judes Av. B80: Stud	6C 32
St Laurence Cl. B48: A'chu	1H 21
St Luke's Cotts. B97: Redd	1F 31
St Martin's Av. B80: Stud	6D 32
St Mary's Ringway DY10: Kidd	4D 6
St Mary's Rd. B49: Alc	4D 36
WR9: Droit S	4E 25
St Michael's Cl. DY13: Stour S	2A 14
St Michael's Ct. DY13: Stour S	2A 14
(off Church Av.)	
St Michael's Pl. DY11: Kidd	3H 5
St Nicholas Cl. B49: Alc	4C 36
St Nicholas St. WR9: Droit S	3D 24
St Oswalds Cl. DY13: Stour S	2F 7
St Patricks Cl. DY11: Kidd	3B 10
St Paul's Av. DY11: Kidd	4A 6
St Peter's Chu. La. WR9: Droit S	4F 25
St Peters Cl. B61: B'gve	3B 22
B97: Redd	5G 31
DY10: Kidd	2E 11
St Peters Ct. B61: B'gve	3B 22
(off St Peters Cl.)	
St Peter's Cres. WR9: Droit S	4F 25
St Peter's Gdns. WR9: Droit S	3F 25
(off St Peter's Wlk.)	
St Peter's Rd. WR9: Droit S	4E 25
St Peter's Wlk. WR9: Droit S	3F 25
St Richard's Gdns. WR9: Droit S	3D 24
St Saviour's Ct. DY9: Hag	2G 17
St Stephen's Gdns. B98: Redd	3H 27
Salford Cl. B98: Redd	4B 32
Salisbury Dr. DY11: Kidd	4H 5
Salop Rd. B97: Redd	6F 27
Saltbarrow Mkt. WR9: Droit S	3E 25
(off High St.)	
Salters Ct. WR9: Had	4H 25
Salter's La. B97: Redd	4C 26
Salters Shop. Cen. WR9: Droit S	3E 25
Saltway WR9: Droit S	3E 25
SALWARPE	5A 24
Salwarpe Rd. B60: B'gve	4B 22
WR9: Droit S	3D 24
SAMBOURNE	3D 34
Sambourne La. B49: Cou	5E 35
B96: A'wd B, Sam	3A 34
B96: Sam	5E 35

Sambourne Pk. B96: Sam	3C 34
Sampson Ct. B61: B'gve	2C 22
(off Worcester Rd.)	
Samsara Rd. B60: B'gve	3F 23
Sandalwood DY10: Kidd	5G 7
(off Comberton Rd.)	
Sandbourne Dr. DY12: Bew	1E 9
Sandbourne La. DY12: Bew	1C 24
Sanderling Ct. DY10: Kidd	3G 11
Sanders Cl. B97: Redd	4C 26
Sanderson Ct. DY11: Kidd	5C 6
Sanders Rd. B61: B'gve	3B 22
Sanders Rd. Ind. Est. B61: B'gve	3B 22
Sandhills Grn. B45: B Grn	2F 21
B48: A'chu	2F 21
Sandhills La. B45: B Grn	3E 21
Sandhills Rd. B45: B Grn	2E 21
Sandhurst Cl. B98: Redd	2C 28
Sandicliffe Cl. DY11: Kidd	2C 6
Sandles Cl. WR9: Droit S	6B 24
Sandles Rd. WR9: Droit S	6B 24
Sandmartin Way DY10: Kidd	2G 11
Sandon Cl. B98: Redd	5A 28
Sandown Dr. B61: Cats	1E 19
Sandpiper Cl. DY10: Kidd	2H 11
Sandstone Rd. DY12: Bew	1E 9
Sandy Bank DY12: Bew	1C 8
Sandygate Cl. B97: Redd	6B 26
Sandy La. DY11: Kidd	1H 5
DY13: Stour S	5B 14
Sandy La. Ind. Est. DY13: Stour S	6B 14
Santa Maria Way DY13: Stour S	3B 14
Santridge Ct. B61: B'gve	6D 18
(off Bewell Head)	
Santridge La. B61: B'gve	6D 18
Sapphire Cl. B60: B'gve	5E 23
Sarah Seager Cl. DY13: Stour S	6G 9
Sarai Cl. WR9: Droit S	6B 24
Saxifrage Pl. DY10: Kidd	1F 11
Saxilby Pl. DY13: Stour S	2B 14
Saxon Cl. B80: Stud	5E 33
Scaife Rd. B60: B'gve	5E 23
Scarfield Cotts. B48: A'chu	5H 21
Scarfield Hill B48: A'chu	5E 21
Schofield Bus. Pk. B60: B'gve	5H 21
Scholars Ct. DY10: Kidd	6E 7
Scholars Wlk. WR9: Droit S	5D 24
School Dr. B60: B'gve	2D 22
School Ho. B60: B'gve	3C 22
School La. B48: A'chu	2H 21
B60: Lick E	4E 19
DY9: Hag	2H 17
School Rd. B45: Alc	4B 36
Scotlands, The WR9: Droit S	1C 24
Scott Rd. B97: Redd	2E 31
Sculthorpe Rd. DY10: Blak	6A 16
Seacole Ho. B97: Redd	6D 26
Sedge Dr. B61: B'gve	4D 18
Sedgefield Wlk. B61: Cats	1C 19
Sedgley Cl. B98: Redd	4H 27
Seedgreen Cl. DY13: Stour S	6G 13
Seggs La. B49: Alc	5B 36
Selba Dr. DY11: Kidd	4H 5
Selsdon Cl. DY11: Kidd	5B 6
Serin Cl. DY10: Kidd	3G 11
Serpentine, The DY11: Kidd	6C 6
Sevenacres La. B98: Redd	3C 28
Sevenhills Dr. DY13: Stour S	6F 13
Severn Bank Pk. DY13: Bew	5D 8
Severn Cl. B61: Cats	2D 18
Severn Cl. B49: Kinw	2D 36
WR9: Droit S	3E 25
Severndale WR9: Droit S	5C 24
Severn Gro. DY11: Kidd	1B 10
Severn Manor Gdns. DY13: Stour S	5G 13
Severn Quay DY12: Bew	1D 8
Severn Ri. DY13: Stour S	1G 13
Severn Rd. DY13: Stour S	4A 14
Severn Side DY13: Stour S	4A 14
Severnside Bus. Pk. DY13: Stour S	5H 14
Severnside Cvm. Pk. DY13: Stour S	5B 14
Severnside Mill DY12: Bew	1D 8
Severn Side Nth. DY12: Bew	1D 8
Severn Side Sth. DY12: Bew	1D 8
Severn Valley Railway	
Bewdley Station	1E 9
Kidderminster Town Station	5F 7
Northwood Halt Station	3B 4
Severn Vw. DY13: Stour S	3A 14
Severn Way DY12: Bew	2B 8
Seymour Dr. B98: Redd	3A 28
Seymour Rd. B49: Alc	3C 36
DY11: Kidd	2B 6
Shaftesbury Cl. B60: B'gve	2E 23
Shakels Cl. B97: Redd	6G 31
Shakespeare Av. B98: Redd	6G 31
Shakespeare Dr. DY10: Redd	4H 7
Shaw Av. DY10: Kidd	4H 7
Shawbank Rd. B98: Redd	5B 28
Shawbury Cl. B98: Redd	5E 29
Shaw Hedge Rd. DY12: Bew	6E 5
Shaws Cl. B97: Redd	6B 26
Shearwater Cl. DY10: Kidd	3H 11
Sheepcote Grange B61: B'gve	5C 18
Sheepcroft Cl. B97: Redd	6B 26
Sheldon Rd. B98: Redd	1A 32
Shelduck Gro. DY10: Kidd	1H 11

Shelley Av. DY10: Kidd	3E 7
Shelley Cl. B61: Cats	2D 18
B97: Redd	2E 31
Sheltwood Cl. B97: Redd	6C 26
Shenstone Cl. B60: B'gve	1D 22
Shenstone Ct. B60: B'gve	1E 23
Shepherds Cl. WR9: Droit S	1C 24
Shepherds Cl. WR0: Droit S	1C 24
(off Shepherds Hill)	
Shepherds Grn. WR9: Droit S	1D 24
Shepherds Hill WR9: Droit S	1C 24
Shepherds Pl. WR9: Droit S	1D 24
Shepherds Ri. WR9: Droit S	1C 24
(off Shepherds Cl.)	
Shepherds Wlk. B60: B'gve	5B 22
Shepherds Way WR9: Droit S	1C 24
Shepley Mdw. B45: B Grn	2C 20
Shepley Rd. B45: B Grn	3B 20
Sheraton Dr. DY10: Kidd	4H 7
Sheraton Rd. B60: B'gve	3F 23
Sherbourne Cl. B98: Redd	6D 28
Sherwell Dr. B49: Alc	4B 36
Sherwood Rd. B60: B'gve	5D 22
Shipston Cl. B97: Redd	4C 26
Shirehampton Cl. B97: Redd	6B 26
Shireland La. B97: Redd	5C 25
Shire Way WR9: Droit S	5G 25
Shirley Jones Cl. B97: Redd	3D 24
Shirley Rd. WR9: Droit S	5B 24
Shottery Cl. B98: Redd	6C 28
Showell Cl. WR9: Droit S	6A 24
Showell Grn. WR9: Droit S	6A 24
Showell Gro. WR9: Droit S	6A 24
Showell Rd. WR9: Droit S	6D 24
Shrawley Av. DY11: Kidd	1B 10
Shrewsbury Rd. DY11: Kidd	5A 6
Shrubbery Cl. DY10: Kidd	3F 7
Shrubbery Gdns. DY10: Kidd	3F 7
Shrubbery Rd. B61: B'gve	3B 22
Shrubbery St. DY10: Kidd	3F 7
SIDEMOOR	6B 18
Sidings, The DY8: Hag	2F 17
Sidings Cl. B60: B'gve	6E 23
Sillins Av. B98: Redd	5A 28
Sillins La. B97: Elc E, Redd	4A 30
Silver Birch Ct. DY10: Kidd	6G 7
(off Oldnall Rd.)	
Silver Birch Dr. DY10: Kidd	5H 7
Silver Birches Bus. Pk. DY10: Kidd	6C 22
Silverdale B61: B'gve	6C 18
Silverstone Av. DY11: Kidd	1D 6
Silver St. B97: Redd	5G 27
Silverwoods Way DY11: Kidd	2C 10
Singer Hill WR9: Droit S	4C 24
(off Bower Hill)	
Sion Av. DY10: Kidd	1F 7
Sion Gdns. DY13: Stour S	3H 13
(not continuous)	
Sion Hill DY10: Kidd, W'ley	1F 7
Sion Hill Ho. DY10: W'ley	1F 7
Sir George's Mall DY10: Kidd	4E 7
Sir Walters Mall DY10: Kidd	4E 7
Siskin Way DY10: Kidd	3H 11
Skilts Av. B98: Redd	1H 31
Skylark Way DY10: Kidd	2G 11
Slad, The DY13: Stour S	6D 10
SLIDESLOW	2F 23
Slideslow Av. B60: B'gve	2E 23
Slideslow Dr. B60: B'gve	1E 23
Slimbridge Cl. B98: Redd	5G 31
Slough, The B80: Stud	5G 31
B97: Redd	5G 31
SMALLWOOD	5G 27
Smallwood Almshouses B98: Redd	5G 27
Smallwood Arch B98: Redd	4G 27
(off Herbert St.)	
Smallwood St. B98: Redd	5G 27
Smith St. B98: Redd	4G 27
Smiths Way B49: Alc	3C 36
Snake La. B48: A'chu	4H 21
Snakes Lake La. B61: D'frd	4A 18
Snake Ter. B48: A'chu	4H 21
Snowberry Cl. DY13: Stour S	2G 13
Snowdon Cl. DY11: Kidd	1C 6
Snowshill Cl. B98: Redd	2B 28
Snuff Mill Wlk. DY12: Bew	2C 8
Somerleyton Av. DY10: Kidd	5G 7
Somerleyton Cl. DY10: Kidd	5G 7
Somerset Dr. DY11: Kidd	1C 6
Sonata Rd. B60: B'gve	3F 23
Soudan B97: Redd	6F 27
Southall Dr. DY11: Hartl	5G 15
South Cres. B60: B'gve	3D 22
SOUTHCREST	1E 31
Southcrest Gdns. B97: Redd	1F 31
Southcrest Rd. B98: Redd	6H 27
Southcrest Rd. DY9: Hag	4F 17
Southgate Cl. DY11: Kidd	6A 6
Southlands Ct. B97: Redd	1E 31
Southmead Cres. B98: Redd	5H 27
Southmead Dr. B60: Lick E	4E 19
Southmead Gdns. B80: Stud	1G 35
Sth. Moons Moat Ind. Area B98: Redd	4D 28
South Pk. Dr. DY13: Stour S	2C 24
South Rd. B60: B'gve	5E 23
DY9: Hag	4F 17

South St. B98: Redd 5G 27
  DY10: Kidd 4F 7
Spadesbourne Rd. B60: Lick E 4F 19
Spa Rd. WR9: Droit S 4E 25
Spencer Av. DY12: Bew 6E 5
Spencer St. DY11: Kidd 6C 6
SPENNELLS 2G 11
Spennells Trad. Est. DY10: Kidd 2F 11
Spennells Valley Rd. DY10: Kidd 2F 11
Spenser Wlk. B61: Cats 2D 18
Spernal Ash B80: Stud 3H 35
Spernal La. B80: Sper 3H 35
Spetchley Cl. B97: Redd 4E 31
Spindle Cl. DY11: Kidd 1D 6
Spinney, The DY13: Stour S 2C 14
Spinney Cl. DY11: Kidd 3A 6
Spinney M. B97: Redd 1E 31
Spinney Wlk. B97: Redd 1E 31
Spirehouse La. B60: B'will, Burc 5G 19
Spire Vw. B61: B'gve 1C 22
Spode Gdns. B60: B'gve 3F 23
Spring Cl. DY9: Hag 4E 17
Springfield Av. B60: B'gve 5D 22
Springfield Bus. Pk. B49: Alc 3B 36
Springfield Ho. B98: Redd 3D 32
Springfield La. DY10: Kidd 2F 7
Springfields Rd. B49: Alc 3B 36
SPRING GROVE 6G 5
Spring Gro. Cres. DY11: Kidd 1B 10
Spring Gro. Rd. DY11: Kidd 1B 10
Spring Hgts. B97: Redd 4F 27
  (off Mill St.)
Springhill Gdns. B97: Redd 6B 26
Springhill Ri. DY12: Bew 6E 5
Springs Av. B61: Cats 1C 18
Springside B98: Redd 2B 32
Springside Pl. DY12: Bew 5E 5
Springvale Dr. B97: Redd 5B 26
Springvale Rd. B97: Redd 6B 26
Spruces, The DY9: Hag 4E 17
Square, The B48: A'chu 1H 21
Stable Ct. WR9: Had 4H 25
Stableford Cl. B97: Redd 3F 31
Stable Way B60: Stoke H 6B 22
Stadium Cl. DY10: Kidd 6F 7
Stagborough Way DY13: Stour S 1G 13
STAKENBRIDGE 4C 16
Stakenbridge La. DY9: Hag 4B 16
  DY10: C'hll 4B 16
Stallard Cl. B97: Redd 3E 27
Stalls Farm Rd. WR9: Droit S 4D 24
Stanford Cl. B97: Redd 4D 30
Stanford Ct. DY12: Bew 5E 5
Stanklyn La. DY10: Kidd, Stone 5G 11
  DY11: Kidd 5G 11
Stanley Cl. B98: Redd 3A 28
Staple Flat B60: Lick E 3F 19
STAPLE HILL 2F 19
Stapleton Cl. B80: Stud 1F 35
  B98: Redd 5D 28
Stapleton Rd. B80: Stud 1F 35
Station App. B45: B Grn 2E 21
  DY10: Kidd 5F 7
Station Cotts. B60: B'will 6B 20
Station Dr. DY9: Hag 3F 17
  DY10: Blak 6B 16
Station Rd. B48: A'chu 5H 21
  B49: Alc 4B 36
  B60: B'will 5B 20
  B80: Stud 6C 32
  DY9: Hag 2F 17
  DY10: Hartl 4H 15
  DY11: Hartl 4H 15
  DY12: Bew 1E 9
Station St. B60: B'gve 2C 22
  WR9: Droit S 3D 24
Station Way B97: Redd 5F 27
Steatite Way DY13: Stour S 1G 13
Steel Cl. B60: B'gve 6D 22
Stephenson Pl. DY12: Bew 1E 9
Stevenson Av. B98: Redd 5H 27
Steve Roberts Ct. DY11: Kidd 4A 6
Stewart Ct. DY10: Kidd 6F 7
Steynors Av. WR9: Droit S 4D 24
Steynors Cl. WR9: Droit S 3D 24
Steynors Way WR9: Droit S 3D 24
STOKE CROSS .4H 23
Stoke La. B98: Redd 1B 28
Stoke Rd. B60: B'gve 5D 22
Stokesay Cl. DY10: Kidd 2E 11
Stoke Turn Ct. B61: Stoke H 5A 22
Stoneback Ct. B61: Stoke H 4A 22
Stonechat Cl. DY10: Kidd 2H 11
Stonehouse Cl. B97: Redd 1E 31
Stonehouse Rd. B60: B'gve 4D 22
Stoneleigh Cl. B98: Redd 4H 31
Stonepits La. B97: Redd 6F 31
STONEY HILL 3D 22
Stoney Hill Cl. B60: B'gve 3D 22
Stoney La. DY10: C'hll 5D 16
  DY10: Kidd 3E 7
Stourbridge Rd. B61: B'gve, Cats, F'fld, Lick E 1B 18
  DY9: Brme 6E 17
  DY9: Clent, Hag 3H 17
  DY9: Hag 1H 17
  DY10: Hurc, Ism, I'ley, Kidd . . . . .3E 7 & 3A 16
Stour Cl. DY13: Stour S 3A 14

Stourport Cvn. Pk. DY13: Stour S 5A 14
Stourport Marina DY13: Stour S 6B 14
Stourport Netball Dome 6A 10
STOURPORT-ON-SEVERN 3A 14
Stourport Rd. DY10: Kidd 4B 10
  DY11: Kidd 4B 10
  DY12: Bew 1D 8
  DY13: C'wick, Titt 6D 14
Stourport Sports Cen. 4H 13
Stourport Sports Club 6A 10
Stourvale Dr. DY10: Kidd 2E 7
Stouton Cft. WR9: Droit S 2D 24
Strand, The B61: B'gve 1D 22
Stratford Gdns. B60: B'gve 2D 22
Stratford Rd. B49: Alc, Ove G 5C 36
  B60: B'gve 2F 23
  (Bromsgrove Highway)
  B60: B'gve 2D 22
  (School Dr.)
Stretton Cft. B45: B Grn 2B 20
Stretton Ho. B97: Redd 4C 26
Stretton Rd. DY11: Kidd 6B 6
Stuarts Ct. DY9: Hag 3F 17
Stuarts Grn. DY9: Pedm 1G 17
STUDLEY 6E 33
Studley Leisure Cen. 6E 33
Studley Point B80: Stud 5E 33
Studley Rd. B98: Redd 5A 28
Suffolk Way WR9: Droit S 5G 25
Sugarbrook Ct. B60: B'gve 6C 22
  (off Aston Rd.)
Sugarbrook La. B60: B'gve 5C 22
Sugar Loaf La. DY7: I'ley 2A 16
  DY10: I'ley 2A 16
Summercroft DY13: Stour S 6G 13
SUMMERFIELD .5F 11
Summerfield Cl. DY11: Kidd 5F 11
Summerfield DY13: Stour S 6B 14
SUMMERHILL 5A 6
Summerhill Av. DY11: Kidd 4A 6
Summerhouse Cl. B97: Redd 4C 30
Summer Pl. DY11: Kidd 5C 6
Summer Rd. DY11: Kidd 5C 6
Summer St. B98: Redd 5G 27
Summervale Cl. DY9: Hag 3F 17
Summervale Rd. DY9: Hag 3E 17
Summerway La. DY11: Tort 6E 11
Sunningdale B60: B'gve 3D 22
  (off New Rd.)
Sunningdale Cl. B98: Redd 3H 27
Sunningdale Rd. B61: B'gve 4A 22
Sunnymead B60: B'gve 3D 22
Sunnyside Gdns. DY11: Kidd 1A 10
Sutton Cl. B98: Redd 6D 28
SUTTON FARM .6B 6
Sutton Pk. Gdns. DY11: Kidd 1B 10
Sutton Pk. Gro. DY11: Kidd 1C 10
Sutton Pk. Ri. DY11: Kidd 1A 10
Sutton Rd. DY11: Kidd 6A 6
Swaledale Cl. B60: Stoke H 6B 22
Swallow Dr. DY10: Kidd 2G 11
Swallow Pl. WR9: Droit S 6G 25
Swan Cen. DY10: Kidd 4E 7
Swan Cl. DY10: Blak 6A 16
Swan Dr. WR9: Droit S 3G 25
Swan Pas. DY13: Stour S 3A 14
Swans Length B48: A'chu 3H 21
Swan St. B48: A'chu 1H 21
  B49: Alc 5B 36
Swans Wlk. B48: A'chu 4H 21
Sweetpool La. DY8: Hag 3E 17
  DY9: Hag 3E 17
Swift Cl. B61: B'gve 4B 22
Swift Pk. Gro. DY10: Kidd 2H 11
Swinburne Rd. B97: Redd 3E 31
Swiss Hgts. DY13: Stour S 5G 13
Sycamore Av. B98: Redd 6G 27
Sycamore Cl. DY10: Kidd 3F 7
Sycamore Ho. B98: Redd 2H 31
  (off Alder Carr Cl.)
Sycamores, The DY9: Hag 3E 17
Sydnall Cl. B97: Redd 6B 26
Sydney Rd. B61: B'gve 1B 22

T

Tabbs Gdns. DY10: Kidd 3G 7
Tagwell Cl. WR9: Droit S 5F 25
Tagwell Gdns. WR9: Droit S 5F 25
Tagwell Grange WR9: Droit S 6G 25
Tagwell Rd. WR9: Droit S 5E 25
Talbot Cl. DY11: Hartl 5G 15
Talbot Rd. B60: B'gve 5B 22
Talbot St. DY11: Kidd 6C 6
Tall Trees Cl. B61: Cats 2C 18
Tanglewood Cl. B60: B'will 4B 20
Tanhouse La. B98: Redd 1C 28
Tanners Hill DY12: Bew 1A 8
Tannoch Cl. B97: Redd 4D 30
Tanworth Cl. B98: Beo 1H 29
Tanyard Cl. B48: A'chu 3H 21
Tanyard La. B48: A'chu 4H 21
Tardebigge Ho. B60: B'gve 1E 23
  (off Burcot La.)

Target Pk. B98: Redd 5A 28
Tarn DY13: Stour S 4A 14
  (off Severn Rd.)
Taynton Cl. B61: B'gve 5B 18
Teal Cres. DY10: Kidd 1G 11
Teal Rd. B80: Stud 5E 33
Teesdale Cl. WR9: Droit S 5B 24
Teeswater Cl. B60: Stoke H 5B 22
Telford Ct. DY12: Bew 1D 8
  (off Severn Side La.)
Telford Dr. DY12: Bew 1C 8
Teme Av. B71: Kidd 1B 10
Teme Cres. WR9: Droit S 6C 24
Temple Cl. B98: Redd 4H 27
Ten Acres B49: Alc 4C 36
  WR9: Droit S 1D 24
Tenacres La. B98: Redd 5E 29
Tenbury Cl. B98: Redd 2C 28
Tenby Way DY13: Stour S 6G 9
Tennyson Rd. B97: Redd 2E 31
Tennyson Way DY10: Kidd 4H 7
Terry's Cl. B98: Redd 3H 27
Terryspring Ct. B98: Redd 5G 27
  (off West Av.)
Thames Dr. WR9: Droit S 5B 24
Thane Cl. B80: Stud 6E 33
Thatchers Cl. WR9: Droit S 1C 24
Thatchers Ct. WR9: Droit S 1C 24
Thatchers Grn. WR9: Droit S 1C 24
  (off Westwood Rd.)
Thatchers Piece WR9: Droit S 1C 24
  (off Thatchers Cl.)
Thatchers Pl. WR9: Droit S 1C 24
  (off Thatchers Way)
Thatchers Way WR9: Droit S 1C 24
The . . . .
  Names prefixed with 'The' for example
  'The Acorns' are indexed under the main name
  such as 'Acorns, The'
Thicknall La. DY9: Clent, Hag 5E 17
Thicknall Ri. DY9: Hag 4F 17
Thirlmere Rd. DY13: Stour S 6H 9
Thirsk Way B61: Cats 1E 19
THOMAS TOWN 1G 35
Thornbury La. B98: Redd 1C 28
Thorncliffe Cl. B97: Redd 4C 30
Thornhill Rd. B98: Redd 1E 29
Thornhill Rd. Ind. Est. . . . .
  B98: Redd 2E 29
Threlfall Dr. DY12: Bew 6F 5
Throckmorton Rd. B49: Alc 4D 36
  B98: Redd 3H 31
Thruxton Cl. B98: Redd 5E 29
Thurston Ct. DY12: Bew 1D 8
  (off Severn Side Sth.)
Tibberton Ct. B60: B'gve 5B 22
Tibbets Cl. B49: Alc 4C 36
Ticknall Cl. B97: Redd 3C 26
Tidbury Cl. B97: Redd 4E 31
Tilehouse Rd. B97: Redd 6F 27
Tillington Cl. B98: Redd 5E 29
Timberhonger La. B61: U War 2A 22
Timberland Way DY13: Stour S 2C 14
Timber La. DY13: Stour S 1B 14
Tintern Cl. B61: B'gve 3B 22
  DY11: Kidd 4H 5
Tipping's Hill B97: Redd 5E 31
TITTON 5C 14
Titton La. DY13: Titt 5C 14
Todd Gdns. DY9: Hag 4G 17
Tolley Rd. DY11: Kidd 3B 10
Tollhouse Rd. B60: Stoke H 6B 22
Tomkinson Dr. DY11: Kidd 6B 6
Toms Town La. B80: Stud 1G 35
Tontine, The DY13: Stour S 3A 14
Tonyn Cl. B48: A'chu 4H 21
Tookeys Dr. B96: A'wd B 4A 34
Topaz Bus. Pk. B61: Lick E 3E 19
Topaz Way B61: Lick E 3E 19
Torridon Cl. DY13: Stour S 5G 9
Torrs Cl. B97: Redd 6F 27
TORTON 1H 15
Torton La. DY10: Tort 1H 15
  DY11: Tort 1G 15
Tourist Info. Cen. . . . .
  Bewdley 1D 8
  Droitwich Spa 3E 25
  Redditch 5G 27
Towbury Cl. B98: Redd 5H 31
Tower Dr. B61: B'gve 4D 18
Tower Hill WR9: Droit S 3F 25
Towers, The DY11: Kidd 3C 10
Towers Bldgs. DY10: Kidd 4E 7
Towers Cl. DY10: Kidd 5H 7
Town Mill Row WR9: Droit S 3F 25
Townsend Av. B61: B'gve 3E 19
Trafford Pk., The B98: Redd 5H 27
Tram St. DY10: Kidd 5E 7
Tranter Av. B48: A'chu 5H 21
Tredington Cl. B98: Redd 4B 32
Trehearn Rd. WR9: Droit S 3G 25
Trent Cl. WR9: Droit S 5C 24
Trescott Rd. B98: Redd 5H 27
Treville Cl. B98: Redd 5E 29
Trevithick Cl. DY13: Stour S 2A 14
Trianon Rd. B60: B'gve 3F 23
Trickses La. B97: Ham G 6A 30

Trimnel Grn. WR9: Droit S 4C 24
(off Celvestune Way)
TRIMPLEY 1E 5
Trimpley Dr. DY11: Kidd 3A 6
Trimpley La. DY12: Bew 5F 5
Trimpley Rd. DY11: Low H 1E 5
DY12: Trim 1C 6
Trinity Ct. B60: B'gve 5E 23
DY10: Kidd 4G 7
Trinity Flds. DY10: Kidd 4F 7
Trinity Grange DY10: Kidd 3F 7
Troy Bus. Pk. B96: Sam 1C 34
Truro Dr. DY11: Kidd 4A 6
Trust Cotts. B96: Sam 4D 34
Tryst, The B61: Lick E 5E 19
Tudor Rd. DY12: Bew 1B 8
Tunnel Dr. B98: Redd 6G 27
Turnpike La. B97: Redd 4C 26
Turnstone Rd. DY10: Kidd 3G 11
Turntable Av. B60: B'gve 6E 23
Turton St. DY10: Kidd 2G 7
Tutors Way DY10: Kidd 6E 7
Twatling Rd. B45: B Grn, Lick 1B 20
Twiners Rd. B98: Redd 1H 31
Tynes, The B60: Stoke H 5B 22
Tyning, The WR9: Droit S 5C 24
Tynings Cl. DY11: Kidd 1B 6
Tynsall Av. B97: Redd 6B 26
Tysoe Cl. B98: Redd 6D 28
Tythe Barn Cl. B60: Stoke H 6A 22
Tything Pk. B49: Kinw 2D 36
Tything Rd. (East) B49: Kinw 2D 36
Tything Rd. (West) B49: Kinw 2C 36

U

Ullapool Cl. B97: Redd 4F 31
Ullenhall La. B98: Beo 2H 29
Ullswater Av. DY13: Stour S 6H 9
Underhill Cl. B98: Redd 4H 31
Underwood Cl. B97: Redd 3C 30
Unicorn Hill B97: Redd 4F 27
Union La. WR9: Droit S 3D 24
Union St. B98: Redd 5H 27
DY10: Kidd 3E 7
Upland Gro. B61: B'gve 5D 18
Upland Rd. B61: B'gve 6D 18
Upleadon Cl. B97: Redd 4C 30
UPPER CATSHILL 1E 19
Up. Crossgate Rd. B98: Redd 2C 32
Upper Fld. Cl. B98: Redd 2C 28
Up. Gambolds La. B60: Fins, S Prior 6F 23
Up. Hall Cl. B98: Redd 6D 28
UPPER MARLBROOK 1G 19
UPPER MITTON 2B 14
Up. Norgrove Ho. B97: Redd 1B 30
Upton Cl. B98: Redd 5F 29
Upton Rd. DY10: Kidd 1F 7
Usmere Rd. DY10: Kidd 1F 7
Uxbridge Ct. DY11: Kidd 5C 6

V

Vale Bus. Pk. DY13: Stour S 3B 14
Vale Ct. B80: Stud .6E 33
Vale Gro. B60: B'gve 5D 22
Vale Ind. Est. DY11: Kidd 3C 10
Valencia Rd. B60: B'gve 3F 23
Valentines Cl. WR9: Droit S 6G 25
Valerian DY10: Kidd 2E 11
Vale Rd. DY13: Stour S 3A 14
Vallet Av. B49: Alc .3B 36
Valley Cl. B97: Redd 4C 30
DY11: Low H 2G 5
Valley Rd. B61: Bourn 3B 18
Valley Stadium 4E 27
Valley Vw. DY12: Bew 1C 8
Valley Wlk. WR9: Droit S 4C 24
(off Valley Way)
Valley Way WR9: Droit S 4C 24
Vawdrey Cl. DY13: Stour S 5G 13
Vaynor Dr. B97: Redd 2F 31
Venneck Cl. DY11: Kidd 2D 10
Venus Bank DY12: Bew 1C 8
Vera Roberts Way DY11: Kidd 1B 10
Vernon Cl. B98: Redd 3A 28
Vernon Ct. DY13: Stour S 2A 14
Vernon Gro. WR9: Droit S 3D 24
Vernon Rd. DY13: Stour S 2A 14
Verona Rd. B60: B'gve 3F 23
Vicarage Cl. B60: B'gve 4E 23
Vicarage Cres. B97: Redd 5E 27
(Marlpool Dr.)
B97: Redd 5F 27
(Vicarage Vw.)
DY10: Kidd 4F 7
Vicarage Farm Heath (Nature Reserve) 3B 10
Vicarage Gdns. B60: B'gve 4E 23
Vicarage Vw. B97: Redd 5F 27
Vicar St. DY10: Kidd 4E 7
Victor Bus. Cen. B98: Redd 5B 28
Victoria Av. WR9: Droit S 5E 25
Victoria Ct. DY10: Kidd 4F 7
Victoria M. B45: B Grn 2E 21
Victoria Pas. DY9: Hag 3F 17

Victoria Pl. DY11: Kidd 1B 10
Victoria Rd. B61: B'gve 1D 22
Victoria Sq. WR9: Droit S 3E 25
Victoria St. B98: Redd 4G 27
Victory Cl. DY13: Stour S 4B 14
VILLAGE, THE 4F 15
Villoneuve M. DY13: Stour S 3A 14
Villiers Rd. B60: B'gve 5A 22
Villiers St. DY10: Kidd 5G 7
VINES, THE 2E 25
Vines La. WR9: Droit S 2E 25
(not continuous)
Vines M. WR9: Droit S 2E 25
Vine St. B97: Redd .4F 27
DY10: Kidd 2G 7
Vowchurch Cl. B97: Redd 3C 26
Vue Cinema
Redditch 5F 27

W

Wadbury Hill B97: Redd 6F 31
Waggoners Cl. B60: Stoke H 6B 22
Waggon La. DY10: Blak, C'hll, Hurc 5A 16
Wain Cl. B49: Alc 3D 36
Wakefield Way B49: Kinw 3D 36
Waldron M. DY9: Hag 3G 17
Walford Wlk. B97: Redd 5G 27
(off Kingfisher Shop. Cen.)
Walker Dr. DY10: Kidd 1G 7
Walkers Rd. B98: Redd 2E 29
WALKWOOD 4E 31
Walkwood Cres. B97: Redd 4E 31
Walkwood Rd. B97: Redd 4E 31
Walnut Gro. DY13: Stour S 2C 14
Walnut La. B60: Fins 4G 23
WALSHES 5H 13
Walshes Farm Cvn. Pk. DY13: Stour S 4H 13
Walter Nash Rd. E. DY11: Kidd 3A 10
Walter Nash Rd. W. DY11: Kidd 3A 10
Walter Stranz Sq. B97: Redd 5G 27
(off Alcester St.)
B98: Redd 5G 27
(off Alcester St.)
Waltham Cl. B61: B'gve 3B 22
Walton Cl. B98: Redd 5E 29
DY11: Kidd 2B 10
DY13: Stour S .5F 13
Walton Rd. B61: B'gve 6E 19
DY10: Hartl 4H 15
Wannerton Rd. DY10: Blak 6A 16
WAPPING
B80 . . . . .5D 32
B98 . . . . .2H 29
Wapping La. B98: Beo 1H 29
Warbank Cl. B48: A'chu 4H 21
Warbler Pl. DY10: Kidd 2G 11
WARESLEY 6G 15
Waresley Ct. Rd. DY11: Hartl 5G 15
Waresley Ho. Mans. DY11: Ware 6H 15
WARESLEY PARK 5G 15
Waresley Pk. DY11: Ware 6G 15
Waresley Rd. DY11: Hartl, Ware 5G 15
Warmstry Rd. B60: B'gve 3G 23
Warstone Cl. DY12: Bew 6F 5
Warstone Mdws. DY12: Bew 5F 5
Warwick Av. B60: B'gve 5D 22
Warwick Cl. B80: Stud 1F 35
Warwick Hall Gdns. B60: B'gve 4D 22
Warwick Highway B80: Map G 6D 28
B98: Redd 2H 31
Warwick St. DY13: Stour S 1A 14
WASHFORD 2E 33
Washford Dr. B98: Redd 3C 32
Washford Ind. Est. B98: Redd 2E 33
Washford La. B98: Redd 2D 32
Washford Trade Pk. B98: Redd 3C 32
Wassell Dr. DY12: Bew 6E 5
Watchtower Rd. DY13: Stour S 6D 10
Watercress Dr. B61: Cats 2C 18
Waterfall Ho. DY13: Stour S 3A 14
(off Waters Edge)
Waterfront Vw. DY13: Stour S 3A 14
Waterlaide Cl. DY11: Hartl 4G 15
Waterlaide Rd. DY11: Hartl 4G 15
Waterloo Dr. DY12: Bew 2B 8
Waterloo St. DY10: Kidd 4E 7
Waters Edge DY13: Stour S 4A 14
Waterside WR9: Droit S 3F 25
Waterside Cl. WR9: Droit S 2F 25
Waterside Grange DY10: Kidd 2E 7
Watery La. B98: Redd 1A 32
DY13: Stour S .4B 14
Watt Cl. B61: B'gve .3C 22
Watt Ct. DY13: Stour S 1A 14
Wattes Cl. B48: A'chu 1H 21
Watts Rd. B80: Stud 2G 35
Waveney Rd. WR9: Droit S 1B 24
Waverley Cl. DY10: Kidd 2F 7
Waycroft DY11: Kidd 4A 10
Weatheroak Cl. B97: Redd 1C 30
Weatheroak Rd. B49: Alc 4D 36
Weaver Cl. WR9: Droit S 3F 25
Weavers Cl. B97: Redd 6F 31
Weavers Hill B97: Redd 6F 31

Weavers Wharf DY10: Kidd 4D 6
WEBHEATH 1C 30
Wedgberrow Cl. WR9: Droit S 4E 25
Weethley Ho. B97: Redd 4C 26
(off Lock Cl.)
Weights La. B97: Redd 1D 26
Weights La. Bus. Pk. B97: Redd 1E 27
Woldock Dr. DY11: Kidd 5B 6
Welch Ga. DY12: Bew 1C 8
Welcome Dr. B61: Cats 1D 18
Welford Cl. B98: Redd 5H 31
Welland Cl. WR9: Droit S 5C 24
Well Cl. B97: Redd 5G 31
Wellesbourne Cl. B98: Redd 4G 27
Wellington Cl. DY11: Kidd 5C 6
Wellington Rd. B60: B'gve 4D 22
Wellington St. B98: Redd 4G 27
Well La. B60: B'gve .2D 22
Wells Cl. DY11: Kidd 4A 6
Wendron Cl. B98: Redd 2E 23
Wendron Gordon Ho. B60: B'gve 3C 22
Wenlock Dr. B61: B'gve 5D 18
Wenlock Way DY13: Stour S 5G 13
Wensleydale WR9: Droit S 5C 24
Wentworth Dr. B60: B'wll 5B 20
Wesley Av. DY13: Stour S 5G 13
Wesley Wlk. B60: B'gve 5B 22
WESTACRE 2D 24
West Av. B98: Redd .5G 27
West Bank WR9: Droit S 1D 24
Westbourne Cl. B61: B'gve 3B 22
Westbourne St. DY12: Bew 1D 8
Westbourne Ter. B61: B'gve 3B 22
Westbury Av. WR9: Droit S 5B 24
Westbury Ct. WR9: Droit S 5B 24
(off New Chawson La.)
Westbury Pl. B98: Redd 2B 32
Westcott Rd. DY10: Kidd 2E 7
West Ct. B60: B'gve .6C 22
Westcroft St. WR9: Droit S 3D 24
(off Ombersley Way)
Westcroft St. WR9: Droit S 3E 25
Western Hill Cl. B96: A'wd B 3A 34
Western Rd. DY9: Hag 4F 17
Western Way DY11: Kidd 5A 6
Westfields B61: Cats 2C 18
WEST HAGLEY 3F 17
West Pk. Dr. WR9: Droit S 2C 24
W. Point Dr. B80: Stud 4D 32
West Rd. B60: B'gve .3D 22
West Stone WR9: Droit S 1D 24
West St. B98: Redd .5G 27
WR9: Droit S 3D 24
West Vw. B60: Marlb 1G 19
Westville Av. DY11: Kidd 5A 6
Westwood Av. WR9: Droit S 5E 25
Westwood Cl. WR9: Droit S 4B 24
Westwood Ho. WR9: Westw 2A 24
WESTWOOD PARK 2A 24
Westwood Rd. WR9: Droit S 2C 24
Westwood Way WR9: Droit S 4A 24
Wey Cl. WR9: Droit S 3F 25
Wey Pl. WR9: Droit S 4C 24
(off Wey Cl.)
Wharfedale Cres. WR9: Droit S 5B 24
Wharral Cl. B98: Redd 2C 28
Wharrage Rd. B49: Alc 4D 36
Wharrington Cl. B98: Redd 2A 32
Wharrington Hill B98: Redd 2A 32
Wharton Pk. Golf Course 3A 8
Wheatcroft Av. DY12: Bew 6E 5
Wheatcroft Cl. B97: Redd 3C 26
Wheatmill Cl. DY10: Blak 6A 16
Wheatridge Rd. B60: Stoke H 6A 22
Wheelers La. B97: Redd 2D 26
Wheeley Rd. B48: A'chu 6D 20
Wheelwright Cl. B60: B'gve 3C 22
Whimbrel Gro. DY10: Kidd 3G 11
Whinchat Gro. DY10: Kidd 2G 11
Whitburn Cl. DY11: Kidd 5B 6
Whitchurch Cl. B98: Redd 4H 31
Whitegate Dr. DY11: Kidd 1A 10
White Heart Cl. DY12: Bew 1B 8
Whitehill Rd. DY11: Kidd 1A 10
White Ho. Dr. B45: B Grn 1B 20
Whitehouse La. B98: Redd 5E 29
Whitenhurst Rd. DY10: Kidd 6D 6
Whitemoor La. B96: Sam 6C 34
Whitford Gdns. B61: B'gve 2A 22
Whitford Rd. B61: B'gve 2A 22
(not continuous)
Whitlenge La. DY10: Hartl 4H 15
Whittall Dr. E. DY11: Kidd 3B 10
Whittall Dr. W. DY11: Kidd 3A 10
Whittingham Ct. WR9: Droit S 3E 25
Whittingham Ho. WR9: Droit S 3F 25
(off Worcester Rd.)

Whittles Ct. DY11: Kidd 2B 6
Whitville Cl. DY11: Kidd 3C 6
Wickham Rd. B80: Stud 6F 33
Widney Ho. Ind. Pk. B97: Redd 4E 27
Wike La. B96: Sam 4E 35
WILDEN 6D 10
Wilden Ind. Est. DY13: Stour S 6C 10
Wilden La. DY10: Kidd 5D 10
   DY11: Kidd 5D 10
   DY13: Stour S 2C 14
Wilden Top Rd. DY13: Stour S 2D 14
Wild Goose La. B98: Redd 1D 32
Wildmoor La. B61: Cats, Wild 1D 18
Willets Rd. WR9: Droit S 6E 25
William Bullock Cl. DY13: Stour S 3H 13
William Coley Pl. DY13: Stour S 5H 13
William Shakespeare Pl. WR9: Droit S 6E 25
William St. B97: Redd .4G 27
Willis St. DY11: Kidd 5C 6
Willoughby Cl. B49: King C 1A 36
Willow Brook Rd. B48: A'chu 3H 21
Willowbud Ho. B98: Redd 2H 31
                         (off Alder Carr Cl.)
Willow Cl. B49: Alc 6B 36
   B61: B'gve 2B 22
   DY9: Hag 3E 17
Willow Ct. B61: B'gve .1B 22
   DY11: Kidd 2B 6
   WR9: Droit S 2C 24
Willowdene DY13: Stour S 3B 14
Willow Dr. WR9: Droit S 6E 25
Willowfield Dr. DY11: Kidd 2C 6
Willow Gdns. B61: B'gve 1B 22
Willow Rd. B61: B'gve .1B 22
Willows, The DY13: Stour S 3C 14
Willow Tree Dr. B45: B Grn 2E 21
Willow Way B80: Stud .2G 35
   B97: Redd 4D 26
Wilmcote Cl. B61: B'gve 4A 22
Wilmcote Ho. B97: Redd 4C 26
                         (off Cardy Cl.)
Wilson Cl. B97: Redd .1E 31
Wilson Ho. DY9: Hag 4G 17
Wilson Rd. DY11: Hartl 5G 15
Wilton Av. DY11: Kidd .3A 6
                     (not continuous)
Winbrook DY12: Bew 1C 8
Winbrook M. DY12: Bew 1C 8
Winchcombe Rd. B49: Alc 4D 36
Winchester Av. DY11: Kidd 4A 6
Winchester Cl. DY9: Hag 2F 17
Windermere DY13: Stour S 3A 14
                    (off Waters Edge)
Windermere Ho. DY10: Kidd 3E 7
Windermere Way DY13: Stour S 6G 9
Windmill Cl. DY13: Stour S 5H 13
Windmill Dr. B97: Redd 4E 31
Windmill Gdns. B97: Redd 4C 30
Windmill La. B97: Redd 4D 30
Windrush Cl. B97: Redd 4F 31
Windsor Ct. B97: Redd 4F 27
Windsor Dr. DY10: Kidd 3E 7
   DY13: Stour S 6H 13
Windsor Gdns. B60: B'gve 2D 22
Windsor Rd. B97: Redd 3F 27
   WR9: Droit S 6E 25
Windsor St. B60: B'gve 2C 22
   B97: Redd 4F 27
Winds Point DY9: Hag .2F 17
Winforton Cl. B98: Redd 5E 29
Winforton Vw. B98: Redd 5E 29
Winnetts La. WR9: Droit S 3E 25
Winslow Av. WR9: Droit S 3G 25
Winslow Cl. B98: Redd 5F 29
Winstone Cl. B98: Redd 4A 28
Winterbourne Cl. B98: Redd 5H 27
Winterfold Cl. DY10: Kidd 4H 7
Wintour Wlk. B60: B'gve 5B 22
Winward Rd. B98: Redd 1F 33
Winyate Hill B98: Redd 6A 28

WINYATES 5E 29
Winyates Cen. B98: Redd 5E 29
WINYATES GREEN 5F 29
Winyates Way B98: Redd 3E 29
                     (not continuous)
Wirehill Dr. B98: Redd .1H 31
Wishaw Cl. B98: Redd .2A 32
Withybed Cl. B48: A'chu 4H 21
WITHYBED GREEN 4G 21
Withybed La. B48: A'chu 4G 21
Witley Cl. DY11: Kidd .2B 10
Witley Way DY13: Stour S 6F 13
WITTON 4E 25
Witton Av. WR9: Droit S 5C 24
Wivelden Av. DY13: Stour S 6D 10
Woburn Cl. B61: B'gve .3A 22
Woodbank Dr. B61: Cats 2C 18
Woodberrow La. B97: Redd 4F 31
Woodbury Cl. B97: Redd 4C 30
   DY11: Hartl 5G 15
Woodbury Dr. B45: B Grn 1B 20
Woodbury Rd. DY11: Kidd 2B 10
   DY13: Stour S 1H 13
Woodbury Rd. Nth. DY13: Stour S 1H 13
Woodbury Rd. W. DY13: Stour S 1H 13
Woodchester DY9: Hag 4G 17
Woodcote Cl. B98: Redd 5E 29
Wood Ct. B97: Redd 1E 31
Woodcroft Cl. B60: B'wll 5A 20
Woodend Cl. B97: Redd 6D 26
Wood End Cl. DY11: Kidd 4D 6
Wood End Dr. B45: B Grn 2B 20
Woodfield Cl. B98: Redd 3A 28
Woodfield Cres. DY11: Kidd 5C 6
Woodfield Rd. WR9: Droit S 2F 25
Woodfields WR9: Droit S 2F 25
Woodfield St. DY11: Kidd 4C 6
Woodgate Cl. B98: Redd 2C 28
Woodgate Ho. B97: Redd 4C 26
Woodgreen Cl. B97: Redd 4C 30
Woodhampton Cl. DY13: Stour S 6H 13
Woodland Av. DY8: Hag 3E 17
   DY11: Kidd 3B 6
Woodland Dr. B45: B Grn 1B 20
Woodland Rd. B97: Redd 5D 26
Woodlands, The DY11: Kidd 1B 10
Woodlands Cl. DY11: Hartl 4H 15
Wood La. DY11: Dunl 4C 12
Woodman Cvn. Pk., The DY12: Ribb 5C 8
Woodmans Cl. WR9: Droit S 1C 24
                   (off Woodmans Way)
Woodmans Grn. WR9: Droit S 2C 24
Woodmans Pl. WR9: Droit S 2C 24
                    (off Farriers Cl.)
Woodmans Ri. WR9: Droit S 1C 24
Woodmans Way WR9: Droit S 1C 24
Woodpecker Gro. DY10: Kidd 2H 11
Wood Piece La. B98: Redd 1D 28
WOODROW 3B 32
Woodrow Cen. B98: Redd 2B 32
                     (not continuous)
Woodrow Cl. B61: Cats .1C 18
Woodrow Dr. B98: Redd 4A 32
Woodrow Ho's. WR9: Droit S 3F 25
Woodrow La. B61: Cats .1D 18
Woodrow Nth. B98: Redd 3A 32
Woodrow Nth. Ter. B98: Redd 2B 32
Woodrow Shop. Cen. B98: Redd 3B 32
Woodrow Sth. B98: Redd 3B 32
Woodrow Wlk. B98: Redd 3A 32
Woodside Av. B97: Redd 6D 26
Woodside Dr. B45: B Grn 2C 20
Wood St. DY11: Kidd 4D 6
Wood Ter. B96: Sam 3D 34
Woodthorpe Dr. DY12: Bew 6C 4
Woodward Rd. DY11: Kidd 1C 10
Woolaston Cl. B98: Redd 2C 32

Woolhope Cl. B98: Redd 5E 29
Wooton Cl. B97: Redd .4C 26
Worcester Cl. DY9: Hag 3F 17
Worcester Cross DY10: Kidd 5E 7
Worcester La. DY9: Hag, Pedm 1G 17
Worcester Rd. B61: B'gve 4B 22
   B61: Stoke H 6A 22
   DY9: Hag 5E 17
   DY10: Hartl, Shens 6H 11
   DY10: Kidd 6E 7
   DY11: Hartl, Kidd, Tort 4G 11
   DY13: Stour S, Titt 3B 14
   WR9: Droit S 6D 24
Worcestershire, The WR9: Droit S 3E 25
Worcestershire County Mus. 3F 15
Worcester Sq. B97: Redd 4G 27
             (off Kingfisher Shop. Cen.)
Worcester St. DY10: Kidd 4E 7
                     (not continuous)
   DY13: Stour S 2A 14
Wordsley Cl. B98: Redd 1B 28
Wordsworth Av. B97: Redd 2E 31
Wordsworth Cres. DY10: Kidd 4H 7
WORMS ASH 4A 18
Worth Cres. DY13: Stour S 6F 9
Wrekin Cl. DY11: Kidd .2B 10
Wrekin Dr. B61: B'gve .5D 18
Wrekin Wlk. DY13: Stour S 5F 13
WRIBBENHALL 1E 9
Wychbold Cl. B97: Redd 4C 30
Wychbold Cl. DY9: Pedm 1H 17
Wychbury Dr. DY9: Hag 1H 17
Wych Rd. WR9: Droit S 4D 24
Wychwood Dr.
   B97: Redd 4F 31
Wye Cl. WR9: Droit S 6D 24
Wynn Cl. DY12: Bew 5F 5
Wyre Ct. DY12: Bew 2B 8
Wyre Forest Cemetery & Crematorium
   DY13: Stour S 5B 10
Wyre Forest Glades Leisure Cen. 4E 7
Wyre Forest Golf Cen. .5H 9
Wyre Hill DY12: Bew 2A 8

Y

Yardley Cl. B98: Redd .5E 29
Yarningale Cl. B98: Redd 4H 31
Yarnold La. B61: Bourn, D'frd 1A 18
Yarranton Cl. DY13: Stour S 6G 13
Yarr Mill Cl. B98: Redd .5H 31
Yeadon Cl. B97: Redd .1C 30
Yellowhammer Ct. DY10: Kidd 3G 11
Yeoman Cl. DY10: Kidd .1E 11
Yeomans Cl. B96: A'wd B 2A 34
Yeomans Wlk. B60: B'gve 4C 22
Yew Tree Cl. B97: Redd 4C 26
                           .1B 8
Yew Tree Dr. B60: B'gve 2E 23
Yew Tree Hill WR9: Droit S 6E 25
Yew Tree La. DY12: Bew 1B 8
Yew Tree Rd. DY10: Kidd 5F 7
Yew Tree Wlk. DY13: Stour S 2G 13
York Av. B61: B'gve 6B 18
   WR9: Droit S 5E 25
York Cl. B61: B'gve 6B 18
   B80: Stud 6C 32
York Ct. DY10: Kidd 3E 7
York Rd. B61: B'gve 6B 18
   DY12: Bew 6B 4
   DY13: Stour S 3A 14
York St. DY10: Kidd 3E 7
Young Cl. DY11: Kidd 2C 10
Yvonne Rd. B97: Redd .4E 31

Z

Zortech Av. DY11: Kidd 4A 10

FSC
www.fsc.org
FSC® C021017

MIX
Paper from
responsible sources

Copyright of Geographers' A-Z Map Company Ltd.

No reproduction by any method whatsoever of any part of this publication is permitted without the prior consent of the copyright owners.

The representation on the maps of a road, track or footpath is no evidence of the existence of a right of way.

SAFETY CAMERA INFORMATION

PocketGPSWorld.com's CamerAlert is a self-contained speed and red light camera warning system for SatNavs and Android or Apple iOS smartphones/tablets. Visit www.cameralert.com to download.

Safety camera locations are publicised by the Safer Roads Partnership which operates them in order to encourage drivers to comply with speed limits at these sites. It is the driver's absolute responsibility to be aware of and to adhere to speed limits at all times.

By showing this safety camera information it is the intention of Geographers' A-Z Map Company Ltd. to encourage safe driving and greater awareness of speed limits and vehicle speed. Data accurate at time of printing.

Printed and bound in the United Kingdom by Gemini Press Ltd., Shoreham-by-Sea, West Sussex
Printed on materials from a sustainable source